BODY
TALK

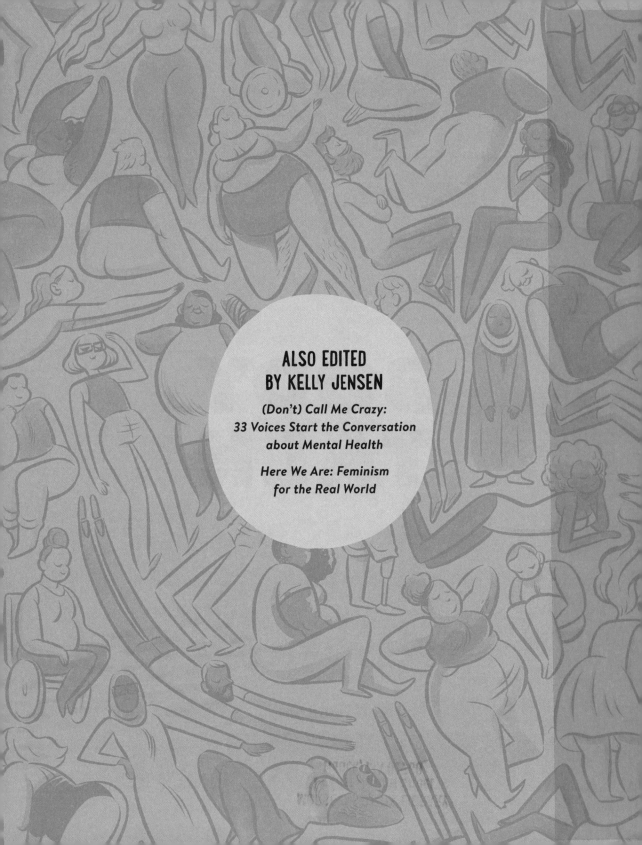

ALSO EDITED
BY KELLY JENSEN

(Don't) Call Me Crazy:
33 Voices Start the Conversation
about Mental Health

Here We Are: Feminism
for the Real World

BODY TALK

37 VOICES
EXPLORE OUR
RADICAL
ANATOMY

EDITED BY
KELLY JENSEN

ALGONQUIN 2020

Published by
Algonquin Young Readers
an imprint of Algonquin Books of Chapel Hill
Post Office Box 2225
Chapel Hill, North Carolina 27515-2225

a division of
Workman Publishing
225 Varick Street
New York, New York 10014

Grateful acknowledgment is made to the holders of copyright,
publishers, or representatives on pages 239–241, which
constitute an extension of the copyright page.

LIBRARY OF CONGRESS CATALOGING-IN-PUBLICATION DATA

Names: Jensen, Kelly, editor.
Title: Body talk : 37 voices explore our radical anatomy / edited by Kelly Jensen.
Description: First edition. | Chapel Hill, North Carolina : Algonquin Young Readers,
an imprint of Algonquin Books of Chapel Hill, 2020. | Includes bibliographical references. |
Audience: Ages 14 and up | Audience: Grades 10–12 | Summary: "Thirty-seven
contributors—including model Tyra Banks, gymnast Aly Raisman, and bestselling YA
authors—explore the world in their unique bodies through essays, lists, comics, and art,
from the award-winning editor of (Don't) Call Me Crazy"—Provided by publisher.
Identifiers: LCCN 2020009794 | ISBN 9781616209674 (trade paperback) |
ISBN 9781643751191 (ebook)
Subjects: LCSH: Human body—Social aspects—Juvenile literature. | Human body—
Political aspects—Juvenile literature. | Body image—Juvenile literature.
Classification: LCC HM636 .B654 2020 | DDC 306.4/613—dc23
LC record available at https://lccn.loc.gov/2020009794

10 9 8 7 6 5 4 3 2 1
First Edition

FOR
EVERY PERSON
WHO HAS WANTED
ANSWERS TO
QUESTIONS THEY'VE
BEEN TOO AFRAID
TO ASK.

CONTENTS

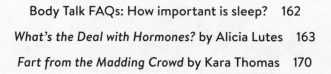

CHAPTER 6

OUR WHOLE SELVES 176

INTRO-
DUCTION

we all experience the world in bodies, but rarely do we take the time to really explore what it means to have and live within them. Just as every single person has a unique personality—shaped both by biology (nature) and by the world around them (nurture)—every single person has a unique body. We may live in a culture that suggests one type of body is the ideal model of what a person should look like and how they should function at a given time and in a given place, but every human body tells its own story, and it's a story we each write for ourselves.

Bodies aren't simply biological. They are radical tools. They are physical and political. They impact our mental well-being as much as they impact our social roles.

Body Talk delves into what it means to operate a body within a twenty-first-century Western world, and offers but one perspective among many others around the world and throughout history. This book goes beyond puberty and beyond body confidence to bare it all.

The late chef and author Anthony Bourdain wrote, "Your body is *not* a temple, it's an amusement park. Enjoy the ride." *Body Talk* aims to throw open the gates to the park so you can better experience the highs, the lows, the thrills, and the chills of the human body.

CHAPTER 1

HEAD, SHOULDERS, KNEES, AND TOES

WE ARE MORE THAN THE SUM OF OUR PARTS.

Whether we have ten fingers and ten toes, whether we have two arms and two legs, whether we've got metal rods and screws holding us together, or whether we have none of the above, there is so much more to having and living in a human body than our particular structure. Our bodies are political as much as they are physical.

This section delves into the ways our anatomy works for us and the ways our anatomy may differ from—or conform to!—the "ideal" human body. It'll also question what, if anything, that ideal is.

SCOLIOSIS, SPINAL FUSION, AND STOMACH PUNCHES

BY RACHAEL LIPPINCOTT

It was ninety-two degrees out, and I was wearing a baggy blue tie-dyed sweat-shirt. It was the only article of clothing I had that hid both my curvature *and* my back brace. So, naturally, I wore it until the white letters were peeling off, my swim team's name wiped from legible existence in my endless pursuit to hide my scoliosis.

This day, though, I was in absolute agony. It felt like a bad reenactment of the first *Pirates of the Caribbean* movie, when Keira Knightley passes out from her suffocating corset and tumbles over a ledge into the ocean below.

Except I ended up crying in the back seat of my mom's forest-green Saturn. The AC blasted as I ripped the Velcro straps open, a waterfall of sweat pouring off my body, like I too had just been rescued from the depths of the ocean. It was there, lying in the back seat while we drove home, that I began to seriously consider if I wanted to keep doing this.

If I didn't continue with the brace, I'd need surgery. A ten-hour spinal-fusion surgery to correct the steadily progressing S-shaped curve in my back.

I had always been a sloucher.

I remember my grandma pulling my shoulders back when I was sitting at her dining room table, telling me about the importance of having good pos-ture, like I were an eighteenth-century heiress at finishing school. I remember my flute teacher telling me over and over again to sit up straighter, my slump-ing making it an absolute nightmare to get any air into my diaphragm.

For the most part, though, I ignored them. It was *exhausting* not to slouch. It took so much energy for me to suck in my stomach and shove my shoulders back that I didn't really see the point in doing it.

Until one day, I saw a picture of what I looked like. And I saw what they'd been talking about for all those years.

It was a low-quality photo, taken on a 2004 Razr flip phone. (This baby was the phone to *have* back in the day. It was the AirPods of the prehistoric era.)

The picture was from the summer before sixth grade. I wasn't doing anything particularly remarkable. Just chilling at my friend's birthday party, wearing an old soccer jersey from the four minutes I played soccer, grinning as I talked about whatever I found interesting as a ten-year-old.

But what *was* remarkable about the photo was that it was the first time I saw how slouched over I really was.

I saw it all. The hunch of my shoulders. The way my right shoulder blade poked out farther than my left. The lower-stomach fat that pulled at the jersey fabric of my shirt, accentuated by the slouch of my upper body.

I felt a disdain for myself that I'm not sure I had really felt until that point. And it was devastating.

It was only a few months later that I had a word to put to the appearance of my back. *Scoliosis.*

I remember bopping into gym class, excited for the usual "Fun Friday" tradition of indoor kickball, and being surprised when our gym teacher rounded us all up for a scheduled back prodding.

It was definitely something a little different for Fun Friday.

We all trotted out of the gym and stood in a line outside the girls' locker room, wearing our orange-and-black gym clothes, going in one at a time to get checked by a doctor. The number of eye rolls was overwhelming. There's nothing quite like a group of impatient sixth-grade girls dressed in their pumpkin-colored gym clothes, wanting nothing more than to be playing kickball but instead having some sixty-five-year-old dude we didn't know telling us if we had weird-shaped backs.

I remember heading into the locker room when "Next!" was called out, my mind already focused on the sound of basketballs reverberating around the gym, this little inspection nothing more than a forgettable pit stop. I followed his instructions, bending over and trying to touch my toes, my arms swinging in the breeze as a display of my unyielding inflexibility.

It's *always* reassuring when you get a sharp inhale from a doctor. I remember him holding the measuring device against my spine, my lumpy right shoulder blade nearly poking him in the eye while he prodded away.

"You can stand now," he said, grabbing a clipboard and scribbling a few notes on it. He tore off a yellow slip and held it out to me. "You definitely have something going on back there. I recommend getting your back looked at as soon as possible."

I trotted out onto the gym floor, reading the name of the doctor he'd referred me to, a nearly illegible note at the top of the slip noting the curvy nature of my spine.

That yellow slip was the start of it all.

The doctor's "You definitely have something going on back there" was putting it mildly. I went to Children's Hospital of Philadelphia and found out that my spine was in the shape of an *S*, like my own body were trying to make a morbid *Sesame Street* alphabet joke. *S* stands for *scoliosis*! Adolescent idiopathic scoliosis, to get really technical.

I had only a twenty-degree curve in the lumbar, or bottom, part of my spine, but a forty-degree curve in the thoracic, or top, part of my spine. Which explained my weird-looking shoulder and why slouching had become a hobby of mine.

I wasn't in pain, but I was well on my way to being in an enormous amount of pain within a few years.

So I got a back brace when I was in seventh grade.

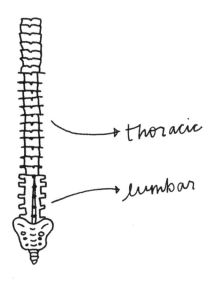

thoracic

lumbar

The intention behind a back brace is that as the wearer grows, the brace literally suffocates the wearer and pushes the spine back into alignment. Or, at the very least, it stops the curve from becoming curvier until the puberty finish line is passed.

Back braces are made of a hard plastic, the inside a slippery padding that does nothing but retain body heat and generate sweat. I was even given these brace-specific knitted tank tops (complete with armpit padding) that were supposed to make the whole setup more comfortable but succeeded only in multiplying my discomfort. Every back brace is different, depending on the type of curvature you have and the severity of the curvature. Since both the upper and lower parts of my spine were affected, my back brace had a curvy U-shaped piece of plastic jutting straight into my left armpit to attack the thoracic curve, and an awkward plastic hip extension that attempted to *literally* press my lumbar spine back into alignment. Three Velcro straps in the back were used to tighten this modern-day corset to a point where my scoliosis just might stop progressing, but it felt like I was one pull away from breaking a rib or suffocating.

Or both, if I was lucky enough.

I had to wear it every day. And every night, ideally. Sixteen to twenty hours per day was the recommended amount of time, and I remember waking up at three in the morning in sweaty, strangulated discomfort, sleepily ripping it off my body in an attempt to savor a few hours of brace-free sleep before I got up.

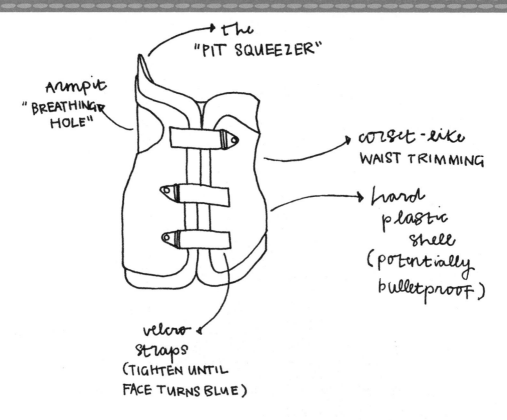

the "PIT SQUEEZER"

Armpit "BREATHING HOLE"

corset-like WAIST TRIMMING

hard plastic shell (potentially bulletproof)

velcro straps (TIGHTEN UNTIL FACE TURNS BLUE)

Don't get me wrong. Wearing a back brace certainly had a few perks. My middle school party trick was letting people punch me in the stomach, because I "couldn't feel it" through my back brace. I'd be standing next to the bounce house at a weekend birthday bash, an unpaid sideshow ready to get an eighth grader's mean left hook right in the gut.

Another perk for me, one that is sad to admit now, was that it made me skinnier. After seeing that picture of myself at my friend's birthday party, I had become a bit obsessed with my weight. Not only was it hard for me to eat a lot with the brace straps tightened all the way, but the constant pressing on my stomach sucked everything in, in a very "Kardashian waist trainer" kind of way. There was even a time after my surgery when I dug the brace out of my closet and stupidly wore it before a first date, hoping to slim myself down before I went out to sit in a dark movie theater where it didn't matter anyway.

Sometimes I wish I could tell my younger self that. That it *didn't matter*. That the body I had then carried me up hills at cross-country meets and through the water during the painful last lap at a swim meet, and that it should be celebrated instead of picked away at and filled with hunger pangs.

I should've gotten both the popcorn *and* the box of candy at the movies that night, instead of sipping away at a Diet Coke from the concession stand.

A few years went by, I grew a few more inches, and I showed up for one of my checkups, hoping that the brace was doing what it was supposed to do, only to find out that it was absolutely not.

The curve in my upper (thoracic) spine had increased to fifty-three degrees, and the curve of my lower (lumbar) spine had more than doubled to a whopping forty-eight degrees.

I felt defeated.

I had essentially worn a back brace for two years for absolutely nothing. I had spent countless nights tossing and turning, unable to sleep, because I couldn't freaking breathe. I had overheated in the summer, cried in the back of cars, and let people punch me in the stomach, hoping that I could just be "normal" at the end of it all. I had started *high school* wearing a back brace, which wasn't exactly a rousing way to start off my social life.

I remember sitting in the doctor's office, feeling *angry*. I barely listened as he talked with my mom about how much worse my back could get. About how much pain I likely had in store for me as I got older.

There were two options. One was to continue with what we had been doing, which was pretty much just pain management and wearing a brace that didn't work for me. And the other was surgery. A spinal-fusion surgery that would span from L3 to T3, thirteen vertebrae drilled through with pedicle screws and connected to metal rods, which would slowly squeeze the spine into the proper shape.

We went for a second opinion at another hospital, St. Christopher's, hoping that we would hear something different. Some solution that didn't include surgery.

We didn't. That orthopedic surgeon even wanted to extend the fusion to T1, in which case I would have had no hip flexibility.

So we returned to Children's Hospital of Philadelphia and set a date. July 8. Ten weeks.

We were handed a thick packet of information detailing the process behind the surgery. The success rate, the failures, the "worst-case scenarios," the "absolute worst-case scenarios." I was even handed a hunk of metal hardware, surprised at the weight of what I'd be carrying around in a few short months.

I don't know why I didn't, but I never read that packet of information. I trusted my surgeon, and I trusted my family. Looking back on it, it was probably a smart decision that I never did my own research. Since then, I've watched videos on YouTube of the process, the physical slicing open of the back and the drilling into the spine, and I probably wouldn't have been able to go through with it had I known exactly what it entailed. At fifteen or sixteen, that blind trust was the best decision I unintentionally made for myself.

The surgery date slowly crept closer and closer. I got MRIs and started the summer swim season. I donated my own blood for the surgery, and I hung out with my friends from school.

And soon it was July 7, the day before my surgery.

I remember being woken up by my mom, surprised when she asked me what I would do if I could do anything in the world (within reason). That should have been an aha moment for me. A moment when I realized the severity of what I was getting into.

But it wasn't.

In Pennsylvania, you need to be sixteen years old to obtain a learner's permit. I didn't have my learner's permit yet, but my last hurrah was zipping around in an empty parking lot, my mom holding the grab handle and trying not to puke.

In some stupid act of bravery, I didn't tell *anyone* about my surgery until the morning of. At five in the morning, in the hospital waiting room, I typed out a quick Facebook post, sending it off for my sleeping friends to discover in a few hours.

It wasn't until I was on the operating table, my eyelids slowly getting heavy, that I felt this raw, overwhelming panic. It was the moment of realization I hadn't had up until that point. A realization that I might not wake up in ten hours. Or that I might wake up *paralyzed*, and all I'd done was send off some last-minute YOLO, tough-kid status update like this wasn't a big deal—more importantly, like the people I cared about weren't a big deal.

I remember lying there and feeling two parts of myself, one screaming at my arms and my legs to *move*. To get up and run before it was too late. And then another telling me everything was going to be OK. That this surgery was a good thing.

Thankfully, the second part won out, blanketing the anxiety in a deep, steady calm as everything around me slowed down and faded to black.

I woke up in a hospital room over ten hours later, the surgery taking longer due to the fact that my three-sport, varsity-athlete bone density was, according to my surgeon, that of a twenty-one-year-old male athlete. I loudly declared to my mom that my back hurt (duh) and that my pain was a solid "7.869" out of 10. I don't remember any of this, but I do remember lying in my hospital bed, being rotated like a chicken every few hours by a lovely staff of nurses I am forever indebted to, the pain so constant I began to see how long I could actually go without pressing the button for the morphine drip.

It was never very long.

I would often get woken up by the sound of my pulse oximeter, which measured the amount of oxygen in my blood, beeping loudly, my mom jolting awake in her reclining chair, her brow furrowed as a nurse jogged into the room to turn it off. I remember having to concentrate really hard on breathing so that the numbers would return to normal, the sound finally stopping as I drifted off to sleep, only to start blaring again a few minutes later. My lungs were getting used to my new spine.

Lung function is one of a few big things to test after spinal-fusion surgery. The shift in the spine is so dramatic that it can affect the lungs. Every hour I had to blow as hard as I could into a spirometer, desperately trying to fill my lungs up with enough air to get that thing to move to where it should be.

The second big thing to test for is paralysis. For the duration of the surgery, there was a neuropathologist measuring my brain waves, making sure that every move my surgeon made with his drill didn't cause any damage. The more I woke up and improved in the days immediately following the surgery, the more tests there were, checking to see if my body still worked the way it used to.

The coolest part was standing. I say this because when I went into surgery, I was an inch and change shorter than my mom. When I slowly stood for the first time post-surgery, we were surprised to find I was now a whole two inches taller than she was. There's a commemorative picture where I'm droopily grinning at the camera, my eyelids heavier than an elephant, my mom beaming with excitement as I clutch her arm for support.

So, truth be told, there *is* a surgery that makes you taller! You just need to have a loopy spine that needs to get ironed out.

And ironed out it had been. After I learned how to walk and go up steps, I was whisked away to get an X-ray, the results of which absolutely blew my mind. For the first time, my spine was completely straight. Like . . . completely. Twenty-one pedicle screws attached to two parallel titanium rods had shifted everything back into a straight line, the likes of which I had certainly never seen before in an X-ray of my spine.

The most incredible thing, though, was not the shift in my spine. It was the change in my perspective.

I became proud of my eighteen-inch scar. I became *proud* of my lumpy shoulder.

I think because of how hard I fought to get better after my surgery, I finally embraced the beauty of my back. There were moments of shock when I showed people my back and my scar, a small part of my journey traced onto my skin. Something I had once kept hidden under tie-dyed sweatshirts and squeezed mercilessly with a back brace was now something I was proud to show off as I strutted onto the deck of the pool at swim meets.

THE MOST INCREDIBLE THING, THOUGH, WAS NOT THE SHIFT IN MY SPINE. IT WAS THE CHANGE IN MY PERSPECTIVE.

My right shoulder blade will always jut out way farther than my left. Whenever I'm at Target trying clothes on and I catch a glimpse of my back in the every-angle-of-yourself-you-never-knew-existed mirrors, I always pause to look at the scar, surprised even after all these years that it's there.

But I feel differently about all of that now.

In a poem my best friend wrote in high school, she called the discolored line down my back the point where an "angel's wings threaten to burst through." I think about that a lot. How the things we so easily label as blemishes or shame inducing or worthy of hiding turn into something beautiful when looked at through the lens of the people who love us.

The most important thing I've learned from this entire experience is that all those things we sometimes don't like about ourselves truly can be seen as beautiful or unique or strong or wonderful if we love *ourselves* enough when we look at them.

There was beauty in my back brace. The *S* of my spine could have been just as capable of inspiring poetry as the eventual scar that replaced it. The fact that I had a slouch when I played the flute made me the most casual-looking musician on any stage.

The parts of us that are different are the parts of us that truly make us special. Oftentimes, they're the parts of us that tell our story.

Love yourself enough to make it a beautiful one.

THE BODY THAT BETRAYED ME

BY EUGENE GRANT

He shouldn't have bent down. Until then, he'd been leaning back against the sweat-soaked ropes of the ring. His feet were planted. His gloved hands covered his face. His head was out of reach of my short arms. His elbows shielded his ribs. Then, perhaps without realizing he was doing it, he threw away the big advantage he had: his height. He bent down. Just a bit. Just enough.

I slammed a left hook into the side of his skull, which was crammed into a blue headguard. The punch didn't knock him out. I doubt it even hurt a lot. But it achieved what I wanted. It sent a signal to him and to those watching us. It sent a signal to anyone who saw someone like me climb onto the canvas and reacted with doubt and amusement. It sent a signal to my opponent: "the dwarf" is no joke. My power was now on record. Don't let me catch you slipping.

As a young man, I didn't consider myself disabled. I had achondroplasia, the most common form of dwarfism, but I wasn't *disabled*. You couldn't be disabled and tough, disabled and manly, disabled and not to be messed with. I, like many other young men, anxiously wanted to be these things. Maybe society disabled me—through others' ignorance and, sometimes, nastiness, and environments that were built without considering dwarf bodies. But I wasn't *disabled* disabled. Not by my body—my silent partner. Together, we disproved the beliefs of people who thought my value was less than theirs simply because I was small. As a young dwarf man, I benefited from all the privileges of being white, straight, cisgender, and middle class. I still do. But back then

I had to work twice as hard as most of my average-height peers to exceed people's expectations.

These expectations were everywhere. They were in our older brothers' magazines, which were filled with rules on what "perfect" male or female bodies should look like. Chiseled. Curvy. Mostly white. Average height. Airbrushed. Nondisabled. They were in our TV shows, on our bedroom posters, in the ads in our newspapers. Galleries of portraits showing individuals with no scars, no folds, no fat, no stretch marks, no wheelchairs, no canes, no dwarfism.

These expectations seeped into our world. We made them our own. They filtered into our classroom conversations, our behavior on the court, our late-night chats when staying over with friends. Testosterone-addled clichés. *Take a punch. Down a pint. Excel at sports. Watch the match. Like these films. Don't cry. Don't be a pussy. Don't care. Don't back down. How many girls have you been with? This is what a man looks like.* We tried so hard to follow these confusing commandments. We tried to stand out—while perfectly fitting in. We tried to be ourselves—while being like everyone else.

These expectations are poisonous to young people, especially those so visibly different from their classmates. When I was a young man, this code of average-height, nondisabled masculinity made me feel like my dwarf body marked me as less of a man. My membership to the club of men was never assumed. And so I spent years trying to show everyone I belonged. I felt I had to be twice as physical to be considered just as manly. I'd hurtle toward the finish line or advance upon an opponent twice my size. It didn't matter if I wasn't the strongest or the fastest. All that mattered was that I was not the weakest or the slowest. It didn't matter if I got battered in a boxing bout. All that mattered was that I gave my opponent, and all who watched, something to think about. And I did it because I felt that the "dwarf" could never come in last, that the crowd wouldn't consider my power to be self-evident, that it needed to be proved.

I loved nothing more than seeing people's eyes widen and disbelief vanish from their faces as they saw what I—a person with dwarfism—could do. I lived off whispered *wows* and the fist bumps of respect from those who now accepted me because I had defied their doubts. At one point, I could run five kilometers in thirty-five minutes—fast, if you remember my legs are half the length of the average person's. My boxing coach told me that pound for pound, I had the hardest punch of anyone he'd trained. I glowed inside.

Through all of this, my dwarf body was my friend. We were literally inseparable. I was as close as I could be to the men in the magazines, the men in the angry crowd on the *Fight Club* poster that once hung above my bed. I was definitely not disabled, I told myself. Even when my stiff dwarf back hurt and my short dwarf legs ached and I needed to sit down because my lower body felt numb and I was tired, so tired in my bones, I was not disabled.

I loved my body. But what I realize now is that I didn't love it on its own terms. Not totally. And if you don't love something on its own terms, maybe that means you never really loved it at all. I thought I loved being a dwarf person. Or maybe I just loved defying people's assumptions about dwarfism without really questioning these assumptions in the first place. I measured my body against the standards our media, pop culture, and social norms drip-fed us. They are high for any young person but nearly impossible for dwarf and disabled adolescents. I can only imagine these benchmarks are even higher and harder to reach for nonwhite, LGBTQ dwarf and disabled teenagers. And while I knew that bodies in magazines and on TV didn't *really* look like that, the result of accepting these standards was that I began to feel they *should* look like that. I'd quietly measure myself against others who were average height and nondisabled. *Sure*, I'd think, *I'm smaller than you, but am I fitter? Faster? Would I have a chance in a fight?* In doing so, I reinforced the same toxic standards against which I was being constantly judged, standards I believed I was fighting.

We live in a capitalist system built on consumption. In this system, bodies—and especially women's bodies—either are used to sell products or are turned into products themselves. Open any men's magazine and you'll see this. They're glossy textbooks prescribing what male and female bodies should look like (and the accessories that the owners of these bodies are supposed to buy). Male bodies are mostly presented as manly standards for men to reach. Women's bodies are mostly presented as sexual objects for men to want. Both are presented as opposites—binary—with no room to maneuver in between. The steps to perfection are also products—the diets, the exercise regimes, the clothes. Altogether, we are sold an entire lifestyle. We are sold a dream.

In this capitalist system, young people are a target market—a group of potential consumers. For consumers to buy a product, they must first believe they need it. And if those products are bodies, consumers must first be made to feel that their own bodies are not enough. Someone who shuns these standards and is confident in their own body is a rebel. Rebels don't fit easily into a system of consumption. That is, unless they can be turned into a commodity, too.

Disabled bodies are not totally excluded from this. Our bodies can be products—just in a different way. This happens in what's called "inspiration porn." Inspiration porn is when people use the bodies and stories of disabled people to present them as "inspiring"—often just for being alive. It happens when disabled people's bodies are depicted in ways that make average-height and nondisabled people feel better about their own. It happens when slogans such as "ability, not disability" or "the only disability is a bad attitude" make it difficult for disabled people to positively identify as being disabled—because we're told disability is a bad thing. And if you're told that the practical barriers you face are "only in your mind," it makes it harder to remove them in real life.

I didn't realize this when I was younger. So I continued to try to achieve standards that were almost impossible. I was "a dwarf *but . . . ,*" as the media so often describe us—a phrase in which the words that follow the *but* nearly always present a dwarf person's ability in something as compensation for their having dwarfism in the first place (for example, saying "they're a dwarf *but really strong*" posits dwarfism as something naturally weak). I did just what society asked of me: I tried to show the world my ability and denied myself my disability. The closer I got to these standards, the more I loved my body.

Until one day, my body betrayed me.

It wasn't long after that bout in the boxing ring, when my opponent bent down that little bit too low, that it happened. It began with what felt like a pulled muscle in my back. The pain made me cry out as I dressed in the mornings. My body was fine, I told myself. Rest and a massage would fix it. Only they didn't. This continued for a few months. The pain shifted from muscular aches—like pulling on a rubber band already stretched to its breaking point— to small electric shocks that buzzed through my lower body. The pain made me grimace. My buttocks and hamstrings felt raw—sunburnt. Almost overnight the cold showers I took (I'd read that James Bond finished his showers running only the cold tap) went from refreshing to unbearable. This continued for a few months. My body was fine, I told myself. Don't be a wimp. Many dwarf people experience nerve pain. Rest and a break from carrying heavy backpacks would fix it. Only they didn't.

I was with a friend when I wet myself, when I realized I wasn't fine, when I felt like I no longer knew my body at all. Later, at the hospital, a series of scans showed the bones in my spine had collapsed and they were cutting off my spinal cord. It looked like black stripes across a smoky white tube. This explained the pain, the rawness, the sensitivity. It explained wetting myself: it was harder for the signals to get from my brain to my muscles when they had to move through my spinal cord. It explained everything, only it didn't. The scans, the surgeon, they all explained *what* had happened, but nothing could explain *why* it had happened. Had I exercised too much? Had I gone too far? They couldn't say—not even a "probably" or "probably not." They didn't know.

Leaving the hospital that day, I walked with a stranger. That stranger was my body. Before then, we'd always shared the same footsteps. But now I knew our paths had separated some time ago. At first, it was only by a fraction, but now there was a chasm between me and the body of which I had demanded so much. I'd built the man I so desperately wanted to be on foundations that were now cracked and splintered. Rubble. I was no longer the dwarf who boxed, the dwarf who ran, the manly dwarf, the dwarf whose value came from disproving others' doubts—there were always doubts, so many doubts—the dwarf who was disabled by society but not by his body. And just then, I no longer recognized myself, for I no longer recognized my body.

LEAVING THE HOSPITAL THAT DAY, I WALKED WITH A STRANGER. THAT STRANGER WAS MY BODY.

My body is still distant from me now. A long scar snakes up my back. It traces the metal that holds my spine together. A short scar creeps up my stomach. It shows where doctors inserted two supports for the metalwork in my back. I can't really bend or twist. This affects everything—from getting out of bed, to dressing, to going to the toilet, to sitting down, to the shoes I wear because I can no longer reach my own shoelaces. I am only truly comfortable when I'm asleep or in the shower. Sometimes my back aches and I can click my rib with a disgusting yet satisfying snap. Weird. I can't enjoy a bath anymore, because my back won't bend to the shape of the tub—instead it stays straight, like a knife dropped into a bowl. Sitting down or leaning a little in any direction causes a dull ache. Some days my hamstrings and buttocks still feel burnt.

Boxing is out of the question—much to my mum's relief. So are the martial arts that I've studied since I was a child and that have helped protect me from the violence that being disabled attracts like a magnet. Perhaps I was so desperate to protect my body from those who would break it that I ended up breaking it myself. I don't know. But I know there are no more whispers in the boxing gym about the dwarf with the left hook. There are no more five-kilometer Parkrun certificates. For the first time, I feel disabled by my body. I am no longer able to impress average-height and nondisabled people with what I can do in order to prove my power, in order to "be a man." For many months after surgery I felt an empty space inside me.

But something has begun to fill this space: a sense of liberation. It's only now that I can no longer meet the standards I've tried so hard to reach, that I have the space to question them. Where did they come from? What do the words *real man* even mean? Who determined this? How did they get the power to do so? Who gave these people the right to judge my dwarf body as being anything other than perfect and flawed and mine and not theirs? Why, in all my years of answering back and questioning, had I never stopped to query this? And if they had affected me in this way, who else had they affected? Had my body really betrayed me? Or, by accepting the standards expected of me and by pushing my body so hard to surpass them, had *I* betrayed my body?

Sometimes standards are used as weapons. They're used to keep people down so others can benefit. They're used to tell those who are down that we're not enough as we are but that we can be enough if we pay for it, if we consume the products, the lifestyle, the dreams we are sold. They turn us from humans—in all our wonderful, untidy difference—into consumers. They're used to build worlds in which white, straight, average-height, and nondisabled men have more power. They're used to build worlds in which women, people of color, the LGBTQ community, disabled and dwarf people, and every intersection between have less power. They're used to enable racism, sexism, homophobia, and misogyny. They're used to present men and women as strict opposites, excluding everyone between. They're used to enable a "gold standard" of manliness. When men believe we're not meeting this standard, we often feel shame, defeat, and self-loathing. This type of masculinity has been directly linked to depression, mental health problems, and suicidal feelings, according to a report from Samaritans (a UK-based mental health charity).

Standards like these—which exclude disabled bodies, dwarf bodies, fat bodies, nonwhite bodies, trans bodies, nonbinary bodies, deviant bodies, scarred bodies, broken bodies—shouldn't be met. Standards that push young boys and men into feeling that they have to be "manly," that they must be this way and not that way, shouldn't be met. They should be torn down. We can start by rejecting what they're selling. We can start by loving who we are and what we already have—ourselves and our bodies. This isn't easy. It's not as simple as flipping a switch. But love isn't supposed to be easy. Sometimes my body vexes me. And that's fine, because it's mine to be frustrated with and no one else's. Like any relationship, sometimes we bicker and argue, but throughout it all, I love my body. My beautiful, broken, scarred, dwarf, and disabled body.

I realize now that my body did not betray me. It did what all bodies do eventually, especially ones we push too hard—it broke down. I realize now that my body is not a stranger to me. Our relationship is just in a different stage. As I grow and change as a person, so does my body. Bodies, like their owners, are complex and messy and gorgeous and weird and changing all the time. I realize now that I *am* disabled, that I have always been disabled, not just by society but by my body, too. And I own that proudly, just as I have always owned proudly being a person with dwarfism. And, as my parents raised me to believe and to know, I have always been enough. I matter. I have value. Just the way I am.

And so do you. Just the way you are.

DO YOU KNOW ABOUT...?

by Eugene Grant

Many people's point of reference for dwarfism will be characters out of films or novels—many of them stereotypes—but do you know about these real-life heroes and role models?

BENJAMIN LAY, one of the first white abolitionists, who campaigned bravely for an end to slavery

PERLA OVITZ, a proud and defiant Jewish woman who survived the Holocaust

JUDY-LYNN DEL REY, a leading science-fiction and fantasy editor and publisher who worked with the genre's most renowned authors

PAUL STEVEN MILLER, an acclaimed lawyer, presidential adviser, and leader in the disability-rights movement

ELIZABETH "ELIZA" GERTRUDE SUGGS, an author in the early twentieth century

JAHMANI SWANSON, a basketball player signed to the world-famous Harlem Globetrotters

What are the best terms to use for disabled people?

Since every single person is different, there isn't one definitive answer to this question. The best place to start is to research what each disabled community prefers. Generally, the disability community likes identity-first language (e.g., *a disabled person*) as opposed to person-first language (e.g., *a person with a disability*). Identity-first language better represents a disabled person's experience moving through the world.

Person-first language is meant to be respectful, but it is rooted in the idea that disability is something negative. It suggests that someone is "more than" their disability, but disabled people note that their experiences are impacted and influenced by their disability. Identity-first language flips the script by acknowledging and respecting a disabled person's experience in the world.

Identity-first language is rooted in the social model of disability, which states that our world isn't built with all bodies and abilities in mind and that it's not the fault of a disabled person that they're limited. A Deaf person isn't limited by the fact that they're deaf; they're limited by a world that doesn't offer accommodations to allow them the same experience as a hearing person.

BODY TALK

FAQS

THE POLITICS OF HAIR BY JERLYN M. THOMAS

AND IT'S FINE

BY KATI GARDNER

Dear Kati,

First, I totally agree that you would be amazing on a soap opera. Like, what's more dramatic than a girl with one leg? It would be epic.

I still love to brag about the fact that you learned how to program the VCR so you could watch *General Hospital* every afternoon. We have dedication to our fandoms. And writing that Liz and Lucky fanfic in 1999 ended up being pretty instrumental in your life. Who knew that someday you'd write a story about a teenager with cancer and it'd actually get published? All because you sat down and wrote a fic about Liz being diagnosed with cancer.

Drama club is tough right now, huh? It hurt to know—to really *know* in your heart—that you would have been perfect in that musical.

It was a hard day, wasn't it? Walking to the theater, passing that trophy case and seeing a reflection.

A girl who had one leg.

And then realizing it was you.

Continuing to the mustard-yellow doors, where, like the parting of the Red Sea, students moved so you could see the cast list, which didn't include your name. It gutted you. I know you cried big tears all over the blue interior of your car. And honestly, it still bothers you sometimes. You weren't crying only because you didn't get a part in the show, but because the people who swore it didn't matter that you were disabled lied.

For that show it mattered. And they said it didn't.

Leaving the cast list, you saw the girl reflected in the trophy case again. The girl with the long brown hair parted down the middle and the wide-leg blue jeans with one whole pant leg tucked up in the back. And your first thought when you saw her? *That girl has one leg. God, that must suck.*

She is disabled.

And you realize in a millisecond that it's you.

You are disabled.

You're not handicapable, physically challenged, or "a cute girl with one leg." Or whatever other phrase you're using these days to lessen the severity for others.

You are disabled, my friend.

AND IT'S FINE.

It won't feel fine when, once again, you see your name next to "Student Director" instead of in the cast. It won't feel fine as you count out the eight counts in a dance audition. It won't feel fine when someone asks a really insensitive question, like how you go to the bathroom, or if you can ever have sex. Yeah, those are coming. Sorry.

But your body is fine.

There's this push and pull. Because you say out loud that it was your choice to have your leg amputated. That you knew it was the best option for you and your type of cancer. And you say all of this with a smile. You explain that even once the surgeons got you into the operating room, they saw that your cancer had decimated the entire femur and there was nothing they could save. You say it was your choice, because there's a lot of truth in that statement. But there are tiny pricks in the back of your brain that always wonder why it all had to happen. That maybe there was something else to be done, but we just didn't know about it. That, god, it would all be so much easier if we just had two legs. If cancer had happened to someone else.

But who?

You could use a prosthesis.

But it's not going to make you abled.

Go back and read those two lines again so it really sinks in.

A prosthesis is just a mobility tool, like crutches or a wheelchair. It's not flesh and bone. It's certainly not *fake*—you're right about that—because it's a real leg that moves people. But it's not organic. And it will not move like your leg did. It is not going to change your status on the census or with the world. They will still see you as disabled.

Kati, I know that you never show the world just how weary you are. Because being disabled can be a time suck. Advocating for basic access. Asking for cups with tops, bags with handles. Defending your need to park in the accessible spots when you're accused of not *really* being disabled and then witnessing the backpedaling when you get out of your car. It's OK to be tired. It's OK.

It's OK.

So you forgot for a hot minute that you're disabled. It doesn't mean anything. It doesn't mean that you aren't accepting of it or whatever. You totally accept that you have one leg. You do think that having the other one amputated saved your life. But here's the thing: the world around you doesn't really accept it. You're young, and people will tell you that you're too young to be disabled. Because obviously, that can happen only when a person is old. Whatever.

You are talented. But trying to convince all these people around you it doesn't matter that you have one leg is so hard. They see only what it takes away, not what it adds. That it doesn't have to be a liability. I think of those productions of *Godspell* that you weren't cast in. I think of what a powerful statement it could have been if the director had chosen to cast you, to have the Jesus character choose NOT to heal you. Telling the world with that simple casting, that simple directorial choice, that being disabled doesn't mean you're less.

There are theaters out there for people with disabilities. They will want you. They will ask you to come and audition. You won't have to work so hard to convince everyone that you're abled. You'll stand on those stages, with those lead roles you so desperately want. No one will forget about your disability, and it will no longer be a liability.

There will be professional shows. Reviews will come in, and one particular performance will be talked about in the Atlanta theater world. It will be noted as one of the best of that year, one of the ones to watch. And in those reviews they will all talk about how you are disabled and how nice it is to see someone with a disability on stage.

You'll be getting dressed, and you'll briefly see yourself in the full-length mirror. And instead of being caught off guard, you'll see a young woman, her one leg wrapped in a spiderweb of tights, a skirt that is way too short, a shirt that shows off her midriff, hair pieces clamped into her now dyed black ponytail. She will look nothing like the preppy, pink-pearl-wearing person you are. But the thought that pops into your head won't be about what she's missing.

It'll be one simple phrase.

This is me.

You have fought every expectation the world has set for you as a disabled person. You climb rock walls, you do high ropes courses, you audition for tap-dancing musicals. You always try to defy the world. To be someone, anyone, but the disabled girl. You're going to grow itchy when people refer to your accomplishments only in light of your disability. "Kati, despite her amputation, continues to . . ." or "Overcoming her handicap, Kati will . . ."

THIS IS ME.

After a while you'll want to be known for what you do. Not what the world feels like you're overcoming. Because it's not like you have a choice. You are doing what you do. You don't want to be special because of your disability.

And I think that's the crux of you, right there.

You want to be seen, to be recognized, but for the love of all that's holy, you want someone to recognize you for something other than having one leg.

That trophy case, where you stood and looked at yourself outside the school theater, is going to linger in your brain for the next twenty years as you navigate the world. You will always be a person with a disability. You will always have a body that's viewed through that lens. And you'll strain against the box the world puts you in. You'll push and fight against the stereotypes of the happy cripple and the depressed cripple, and instead, you will own that you are a disabled person. And that image of the girl in the trophy case will sit in your mind's eye, and when you're older, you'll smile . . . because you can totally be on *General Hospital*. It would be ridiculously epic.

Princess: sparkle and twirl and audition and advocate, but never forget that you are a person. Full stop. You are not an amputee first. You are a person. And your body is what it is. And it moves you; it allows you to be who you are.

I'm not going to leave you with some great challenge to change the world, because that's bullshit. Remember that girl in the trophy case. Remember the young woman in the too-short skirt.

Both are you.

Both are whole.

Sunshine forever, Princess.

Love,
Kati from the Future

BODY TALK
FAQS

what does *accessibility* mean?

Accessibility is the way physical and digital things are designed so that disabled people can use them. Accessibility has two components: "direct access" and "indirect access." Direct access means a disabled person can use something without assistance, whereas indirect access means a disabled person's own assistive technology is needed to use the service or item.

Nondisabled people likely do not think about accessibility in their day-to-day lives. But disabled people do—the label *disabled* itself makes clear the inaccessibility of a world that's been built with nondisabled people as the default. Accessible design anticipates the needs of people with a variety of disabilities and strives to create spaces and systems where disabled people can fully participate and thrive.

Accessible design is not ubiquitous, though, and despite governmental regulations (which differ from country to country and from city to city), it's not a standard of physical or digital experiences. More often than not, the bare minimum is done to meet requirements.

Examples of accessibility include wheelchair ramps on stages, closed-captioning for audio-visual experiences, alternative text for visual content (such as photos) on the web, lowered service counters, signage that uses both text *and* visual icons, handrails along walls, and required use of microphones at events.

EMBRACE YOUR BOOTY

BY TYRA BANKS AND CAROLYN LONDON

Tyra: Everyone thought I was on vacation, just letting it all hang out. But really, I was in Australia shooting for *Top Model* when those photos were taken. People think I got caught during some me time, but child, I was posing. For you.

Anyway, you might know the photos I'm talking about. Me. In a brown strapless one-piece swimsuit, on the beach, my hair's flowing and my ass and thighs, well . . . some say those are ummm . . . overflowing. I call it curvy, thick, sexy, voluptuous. But the world called it something else.

Fat.

During that photo shoot, we knew that there were paparazzi in the distance. My security was trained to recognize the glare on a lens, no matter how far away, and when they saw that signature reflection of light way up in the trees, we knew exactly what it was.

Whatever, we shrugged it off. Paparazzi come with the territory of being in the public eye, especially on a beach. A beach complete with a crew of about fifteen people doing a photo shoot. That #squad ain't blendin' in. We were some busy people, too. We had eight more shoots and locations to go to in Sydney that day, so we couldn't waste time chasing the "paps" off every time one popped up.

After my last shot on the beach, as I was walking back to the location van, a paparazzo had emerged from the bushes and was right in the sand. I said hello, joked and asked him if he got the shot, and I was on my way. I didn't get annoyed until he showed up at lunch miles away from the beach. "Oh, come on," I thought. "Can't this dude go bother somebody else? There has got to be some famous Australian around here somewhere. Where the heck is Nicole Kidman when you need her?"

I dropped some hints to him that he should be done, and he picked up on none of them—not even the one where I straight-up—yet politely—asked him to leave us alone so we could eat our juicy Australian steaks in peace.

He snapped away through the appetizer, main course, and dessert. So, my team and I brainstormed ways that we could have a little fun with him. As soon as we'd paid the check, we put our plan into action. Everyone at our table pulled out their camera phones and we chased him down the sidewalk, snapping away. We wanted him to see how it felt.

We were lighthearted, smiling and laughing the whole time, and the "photo shoot" lasted all of fifteen feet. But someone wasn't smiling at all. My pap was pissed.

"Come on, dude," I said. "It's all love. We were just having a little fun being you." Then I got in the van, and we drove away and had forgotten all about it as we continued to shoot around the city. When I laid my head on my pillow that night at the hotel, I'd forgotten it all.

Two weeks later, I landed at LAX airport and was back in the U.S. of A. I enjoyed Australia but it felt good to be home. As soon as the plane touched down, my cell phone was blowing up. Countless texts and voice mails, asking me if I was OK. Was I OK? Of course I was OK. I'd just spent three weeks shooting *Top Model* and had crowned a cha-cha diva winner who was gonna win the hearts of America and the world.

But then more messages started to flood in. Messages that revealed what the "Are you OK" concerned ones were all about: me on the cover of every tabloid out there, with headlines like AMERICA'S NEXT TOP WADDLE and THIGH-RA BANKS and TYRA TOPS 200 LBS!!! I about died when I saw that—of laughter. I thought it was crazy, but I did not take it seriously. But I did recognize that the people who sent them to me seemed to be enjoying every minute of it.

You don't need me to tell you this, because anyone who's ever accidentally opened their photo to the selfie cam when they weren't expecting it knows—pictures can tell all kinds of cray stories. Oh yes, I was bigger than usual at the time, but it was nothing that was outside my normal "bigger phase" range.

PICTURES CAN TELL ALL KINDS OF CRAY STORIES.

The photos had just come out and people were coming up to me like, "Oh my God, you look great! How did you lose all that weight in a week?" If they didn't know that it was damn near impossible for someone to lose forty pounds in seven days, I didn't consider it my job to enlighten them. I didn't tell people that I hadn't lost any weight at all, that it was all in the difference a paparazzi photo can make. I just tried to brush it off and change the subject. "Oh, well, I don't know . . . but damn, girl, *you* look fantastic. What type of weave hair are you using these days?"

Cut to a day later. I was standing in line at the grocery store. (Yes, I shop for my own groceries often.) The woman in front of me was looking at the tabloid magazine covers, then turned around and looked me straight in the eyes. There was no "OMG, Tyra, I can't believe you do your own grocery shopping!" look on her face. Instead she said, "If they're calling *you* fat, what am I?" And she said it through tears.

That was when it hit me—this whole incident wasn't funny, and it wasn't just about me.

No pun intended, but it was bigger than me. Much bigger.

I called my *Tyra Banks Show* producers from the car on the way home. We worked on producing the response-to-the-tabloids show for about a week, and I had intense sessions with my team of producers to bounce ideas off them and figure out exactly what I wanted to say. (Thanks, Lauren Berry-Blincoe and John Redmann!) At first, I was going to end my diatribe by saying,

"To everyone who goes around calling me and other women fat, f*ck you!" and flip off the camera. When the show aired, we'd just bleep out my words and blur my hands.

Then we sat back and realized that we wanted this moment to be more poignant than cursing, and we didn't want to bleep or blur any part of it out, so we rewrote it. I tried so many different versions, like "Forget you!" or "Kiss my butt," and even called the Standards and Practices, the censor police of network television. "Can I say 'ass' on TV?" I asked.

We had a winner.

The day of shooting, I was dressed in my little talk show dress, looking prim and proper. But something felt off. I called out to my stylist, Yaniece, "Do you still have that swimsuit from Australia?"

"The swimsuit?" she asked.

"Yeah, *the* swimsuit."

"Girl, yeah. It's with all that *Top Model* stuff over there in that suitcase."

"Get it out," I said.

"Why?"

I started taking off my clothes.

"What are you doing?" she asked, looking at me like I was crazier than I already was.

"Just help me put it on," I said.

She helped me yank it up, and I was about ready to exit my dressing room when I thought, "Oh shoot, I may be brave, but I ain't stupid." I called over Valente, my longtime makeup artist, who was also on the Australian beach with me, to put some body makeup on my legs, and run some Victoria's Secret– like shimmer down the front of my thighs (a trick that makes it look like there's a muscle there when there ain't).

Then I walked out the door, straight to the stage.

When I entered that set in *that* swimsuit and nothing else, my staff and many of my producers were as shocked as the studio audience.

Carolyn: I was sitting in my living room in front of the TV, sipping on my daily can of ginger ale, when Tyra strutted onto the set of her talk show sporting the same bathing suit that was plastered on the cover of every gossip magazine around the world.

Of course, she had told me that she was going to address the paparazzi's blatant attempt at public humiliation, but not dressed like that! With every sip, I grew more and more proud.

Tyra: I addressed the audience and was as real and as raw as was humanly possible, and ended it yelling, "Kiss my FAT ass!" Oh, I slapped my own ass super hard when I said "fat," too. I had wanted the whole speech to be strong, empowering, *fierce*. But now, as the audience screamed and cheered and teared up and even sobbed, I realized I was crying, too. What the hell? I was just laughing about all of this a week ago. But now, I was feeling weak and vulnerable. *WTF?*

I needed to be strong. I needed to be a warrior. I needed to be an example to women everywhere that they could survive this body shaming without letting it break them down. I ran straight to the control booth to my director, Brian.

"Brian," I said, wiping snot from my nose. "I started to cry out there. So we gotta do it again. And I want you to end the 'Kiss my fat ass' part with a shot close on my face—strong and defiant. There was this woman in the grocery store, and I can't have her see me all teary. Nobody should see me crying. It's weak."

Brian looked at me—actually, he looked *through* me—then started walking around the booth, turning off each and every monitor. When he was done, he turned to me and said, "Tyra, go home."

"What?" I said.

"Go home," he repeated. "Yes, you cried. Yes, you were vulnerable. But it was real. It was you. And I'm not gonna say it again after this. Go. Home."

So, I did as he said. I went home. I hardly slept for the next two weeks, until it aired.

And the day it aired changed my life forever.

Carolyn: "Kiss my fat ass!" Whew! Those four words that Tyra said—no, *yelled*—were not what I had expected. But I was overjoyed! By the time she slapped her butt, I had leapt off the couch, spilled ginger ale on my shirt, and had tears rolling down my cheeks. Tyra spoke in defense of all of us who have witnessed or experienced the physical and emotional chains that are forced upon women throughout our lives. It was as if she was screaming in unison with all of our voices: "Enough is friggin' enough!" The resounding response from women and girls around the planet said it all. We were tired of feeling that we are worth nothing more than what we weigh.

Tyra: That butt slap was felt everywhere—from beauty salons to office buildings to locker rooms to school playgrounds to damn near every news and online outlet in the darn universe. I saw the gorgeous and talented Adele at an Alicia Keys event and she wrapped her arms around me and thanked me from her beautiful body and soul profusely. Women (and men, too) from all over the world were writing in about how much what I said meant to them. A week later at intermission of the musical *Rent* in NYC, a woman pulled me aside and said the moment saved her life, that she had a handful of pills but experienced that moment and immediately called a suicide hotline that ended up saving her life. *Time* magazine named me one of the most influential people of the year next to Barack Obama, Oprah Winfrey, and Richard Branson (and in the Heroes and Pioneers category, no less). And the speech made it onto *TV Guide Magazine*'s 60 Greatest Talk Show Moments list.

I had no idea it would lead to all of that. But I realized it had this impact because it was a real moment. At the time I taped it, I thought real meant polished. A do-over. Perfection. But if I had delivered that speech how I wanted to—cool and calculated, and yeah, 100 percent "strong," like I wasn't bothered one bit by people calling me fat—it would not have resonated the powerful way it did.

I believe in those words that I said on my talk show just as much today as I did when I first said them, more than ten years ago. And just in case you weren't there back then to experience the moment, and even if you were, I've brought it here . . . to you:

> *I love my mama. She has helped me to be a strong woman so I can overcome these kind of attacks, but if I had lower self-esteem, I would probably be starving myself right now. But, that's exactly what is happening to other women all over this country. So, I have something to say to all of you that have something nasty to say about me or other women who are built like me . . . women whose names you know, women whose names you don't, women who've been picked on, women whose husbands put them down, women at work or girls in school—I have one thing to say to you: Kiss my fat ass!*

Carolyn: This epic moment was a culmination of all that I had worked so hard to instill in Tyra. She had sprouted her own wings and was flying high.

Fat ass and all.

This piece was previously published in Perfect Is Boring *by Tyra Banks and Carolyn London.*

CHAPTER 2

ON THE SURFACE

TEETH. HAIR. BIRTHMARKS. MOLES.

We can see these things because they're superficial, on the surface of our bodies. Sure, we might be able to straighten teeth or cut hair. We can hide birthmarks and moles with clothing or makeup. But what do they mean on a deeper level?

These features can make our bodies unique and fascinating as much as they can make our bodies annoying or frustrating. They tell stories that go far beyond what's seen. They tell us about who we are, as well as where we come from.

THE GHOSTS OF CHRISTMAS PAST, OR WHEN THE ANGEL LEARNED TO SHAVE

BY ERIC SMITH

The year I became an angel was the year I started to shave.

It was during the Year of the Preteen Mustache that some casting directors from Broadway came to my inner-city school to do some outreach and look for young talent. They'd asked some kids a few years prior to be in the chorus of *Joseph and the Amazing Technicolor Dreamcoat*, so hopes were very high among me and my band-, chorus-, and theater-geek friends that we might be picked to be a part of a show, too. I mean, the kids who went on to be in that musical were so cool. We got to go on a class trip to see them once! They were, like, famous!

They weren't. But I was eleven. I didn't know better.

The details that led to me and several of my friends being cast as angels in the original Broadway production of *A Christmas Carol* aren't terribly interesting. There was an audition, followed by weeks of waiting. There were a lot of late-night rehearsals, from which my mom and other parents picked me and my pals up at midnight. Then there were costume fittings in New York City, big white fluffy outfits full of glitter and sequins. Dress rehearsals with bright lights and smoke machines. Passionate musical directors pushing this legion of eleven- and twelve-year-old kids to behave professionally, and the school's chorus directors, two teachers who stared at us with the kind of pride that comes only with this kind of success.

There was even a recording studio, where we all crammed in and sang our collective hearts out for a Nobody Beats the Wiz commercial (I realize some of you readers might not even be aware of that former retail giant) and the original Broadway soundtrack.

That's right. Somewhere in the bowels of your favorite used record store's twenty-five-cent bin of soundtracks on CDs, you might be able to find me singing on a few hot tracks.

As the opening night grew closer and photos became more frequent, I grew increasingly insecure about walking across that stage. In the show, the entire cast of angels would hold hands as we made our way across downstage, standing in front of all the actors, sparkling under the lights to sing our big song. But I couldn't stop thinking about my face. Teachers never said anything to me about it, and none of my friends did either, but I could *feel* it. In their side glances and narrow-lipped smiles. Something about me, the way I looked, was wrong.

"Dad. Dad, I need to shave!" I exclaimed. "I'm supposed to be an angel." Dress rehearsals were in full swing, and opening night was a little under a week away.

"You'll be fine," my mom said. "You're *already* an angel." Yes, my mother actually talked like this, and still does.

"*Mom!* No! I need to—"

"All right, that does it. Upstairs." My dad huffed, getting up from the kitchen table.

Armed with one of those single-blade Bic razors—this was long before the era of the Gillette razors that sound like weapons from a bad fantasy novel, *Mach Fusion 6: The Razor of a Thousand Blades*—my dad lathered some shaving foam on my upper lip. I stared at the mirror, catching my mom behind us, having herself a good cry. I'd learn this would become a tradition, my mother crying over every major life moment.

Graduating from junior high.

Graduating from high school.

Graduating from being an eleven-year-old with a mustache to an eleven-year-old who had to start shaving because he was appearing as an angel in a Broadway musical.

You know, traditional benchmarks for parenting.

I remember being anxious that evening after shaving for the very first time, lying in bed and singing songs from the musical loudly and likely driving my parents and little sister mad. I was excited because I couldn't wait for that first show and because we had school the next day, and here I was, with a new face. Surely with a new face, I was a new person. It felt like a fresh start. How many bullied eleven-year-olds get a fresh start?

Turns out I didn't get one. Everyone made fun of me.

"You shaved!?" A girl (whose name I remember but won't mention here, because I'm a better person than you, BRIANA) mocked me on the playground. "You're a freak."

I couldn't win. I couldn't. I spent that week being made fun of on the playground and in the hallways and at Boy Scouts and on the bus . . . and as opening night of *A Christmas Carol* grew closer, my mustache slowly came back in.

Due to my genetics, a blend of Palestinian, Sicilian, and Honduran, I was blessed with this mustache at the ripe old age of eleven. I'm not talking about a little bit of peach fuzz here. No, this was a legit mustache, like something a freshman might try and fail to grow their first year of college. It was noticeable, and not something that could be hidden under Broadway stage makeup.

I got picked on a lot, for more reasons than just the hair. For looking the way I did, having not only the facial hair but a birthmark that marred the right side of my jawline. For having an unusually simple name as an adopted brown kid, thus frequently raising questions among people who didn't know me. Oh, and for the way I dressed. My parents had a knack for clothing me in single-color sweatshirts and pants, earning me the nickname "the Purple Wolf" from a few older kids, thanks to a set of bright purple sweats that still haunt me to this day.

I complained to my parents a lot about the mocking and the bullying that happened in the classroom, in Boy Scouts, and in other after-school activities. And my parents were great at telling me exactly the wrong thing to say.

One time, when some of these same older kids asked me about all my body hair (my arms and legs are . . . *significantly* covered) and my mustache while shoving me around a bit in the lunchroom, I looked one of them in the eye and said, "Someday when *you're* a man, you'll understand."

My mom had told me to say that.

And when I think about that now, I can appreciate that my mother was a master of the burn and that she meant well.

I got my ass kicked.

Post-shave, with the mustache temporarily gone from my face, things hadn't gotten better. And when the musical finally premiered, it was hard to truly enjoy it.

The months we were on Broadway, I wrestled with insecurity. Some days I had the mustache, because as I quickly learned as a hairy eleven-year-old, I was destined to be one of those people who had to shave every single day, the hair on my face growing back faster than weeds on the sidewalk. Other days I took the time to shave, my dad standing next to me and keeping a watchful eye while I did it, giving me little pieces of paper towel every time I cut myself.

It was an era that was meant to be one of the greatest moments of my young life. Performing on a Broadway stage, with a handful of friends who are still some of my closest to this day. The trips to New York City every other day, on fancy charter buses. The way my family beamed when talking about this accomplishment, especially my mother. She would light up like the Christmas trees we drove by in Manhattan.

But to this day, when I hear kids singing Christmas music as the holidays draw near—those choruses of children—it takes me thundering back.

Suddenly I'm a kid on a bus, full of panic and wondering if I'm ugly or not. Burying my eyes in video game magazines with my best friend, Miguel, hearing the laughter at the back of the bus and wondering if it is about me. Squinting down at the Broadway audience, hoping no one is staring at my facial hair. Wondering if there's something wrong with me, an overly hairy boy who can't decide whether to shave that day and whether to wear glasses during the show.

Just trying so very hard to figure out the right combination of things will make me feel better about myself when thousands of people are watching me sing under beaming stage lights, sequins on my costume shimmering, night after night.

Those body issues remained with me for a long time, and I fought them for years.

I purposefully didn't wear my glasses, making my eyes worse. I shaved almost every single day from junior high until I was nearly thirty, occasionally growing the poor-choice goatee. In high school, I once grew a beard and dyed the ends blond, red, and blue. I irritated the hell out of my skin, both from shaving and from bleaching my facial hair. The chemicals on my face led to awful breakouts, and shaving on that sensitive skin led to razor bumps that still grace my face two decades later. But none of that stopped me. I thought maybe if I just ignored all of that or kept pushing to transform how I looked, to alter my face, I somehow might be happier. Might be accepted.

If I put on a show.

TO THIS DAY, WHEN I HEAR KIDS SINGING CHRISTMAS MUSIC AS THE HOLIDAYS DRAW NEAR, IT TAKES ME THUNDERING BACK.

I feel like I spent years as that kid on that stage. Trying to be what I thought an audience wanted, wrestling with my appearance. Glasses, no glasses. Beard, no beard. I filled most aspects of my life with a desperate need to be liked. To be seen. I was in all the plays in high school and even pushed ahead as a theater major in college. I played in bands. I wanted to know that *all of this*—you can't see it, but I'm gesturing at my face—was OK.

I think a lot of us think we need to put on a show in life. A performance. Maybe it's an act to get a job. A metaphorical social dance to make friends. Maybe it's to fall in love. To look like the person you *think* you need to be, instead of the person you *are*. And I just want to tell you this: Be. Who. You. Are.

I think back to my smart-ass remarks to the kids who picked on me. The words my parents told me to fire back. "Someday when you're a man, you'll understand."

And now I do.

But I still don't want to hear your little brother sing "Jingle Bells."

SIXTY-FOUR TEETH

BY SARA SAEDI

My parents forced me to get braces at the tender and turbulent age of thirteen. I had no say in the matter. They didn't care that the thirty-two (albeit very crooked) teeth resided in my mouth. If I wanted to get married, get a job, have any future at all, I had to fix my smile.

I remember trying to reason with them on the way home from the orthodontist's office:

"I have personality. I don't need to be beautiful!"

"Why do I have to go to an Iranian orthodontist with bad breath?"

"Death to America's obsession with dental hygiene!"

But they were unmoved. It was one of the rare instances in our relationship where my opinion was irrelevant.

Eleven years prior, we'd escaped Tehran in the aftermath of the Iranian Revolution, but when it came to the subject of my teeth, my parents were as tyrannical as the Ayatollah.

"You'll thank us one day," was all they said in response.

I was too respectful (and afraid) to say that I hated my parents out loud, so instead, I repeated the words in my head like a teenage war cry. *I hate you. I hate you. I hate you.*

I'm fairly certain that the status of my dad's teeth never crossed my mind on that drive home. But as a kid, I used to hang out in the bathroom and observe his strict dental regimen. He was religious about flossing, brushing, and swigging mouthwash, but you wouldn't know it from looking at him. For starters, he'd been a smoker before I was born, and his crooked teeth never recovered from their exposure to nicotine.

Braces hadn't existed in Iran when he was growing up. In fact, it wasn't until 1975 that a group of American-trained orthodontists would be invited to Tehran University to train Iranian students. Once advances were made in the field of orthodontics, demand for braces would still outweigh the supply of orthodontists. Straight teeth would become a luxury afforded only to the elite. Dental work was never an option for my dad. And yet, he kept flossing and brushing and swigging mouthwash. He had no intention of giving up on his teeth.

My dad always had a gregarious personality. He's cheerful and upbeat and the type of guy most people love instantly. He may have been self-conscious about smiling with his teeth showing, but it's hard to stay tight-lipped when you're regularly brimming with joy. I love his outgoing side. I love that he talks to the clerk at the grocery store or a stranger on the street like he's known them his whole life. But as a teenager, I worried those same people might judge him at the sight of his stained and imperfect teeth. I worried his mouth was just another sign of our foreignness. I had frequent bouts of anxiety over how different we were from my American friends' families. Anxiety that was compounded by a family secret I'd discovered: we were undocumented immigrants.

It was my older sister who unceremoniously broke the news of our immigration status to me. Despite the fact that we'd lived in the Bay Area for over a decade, we didn't have green cards. At the time, my sister and I didn't even have Social Security numbers. We'd escaped Iran as refugees but entered the United States on visitor visas. When they expired, we applied for political asylum, but after two years, we were told there was no record of our application. Our only hope was getting green cards through my uncle, who was an American citizen. So we filed our applications and waited and waited and waited.

Our undocumented status was the reason I had to go to the Iranian orthodontist with halitosis. He generously gave us his friends-and-family rate for my braces. This was a necessary savings for my parents. Being undocumented came with an array of financial burdens. It meant paying a lawyer to help get my sister and me Social Security numbers. It also meant not being able to apply for financial aid when my sister went off to college. My parents would have to pay for her education in full. For small-business owners, this was a behemoth expense.

Braces were not exactly cost-prohibitive, but my teeth required a lot of work. I had to start with a palatal expander to widen my upper jaw. This is a metal contraption (or torture device) that's secured to your top molars and sits below the roof of your mouth. It has a tiny screw that you turn with a small metal key each day to help move your teeth apart. If that wasn't humiliating enough, it also made me speak with a lisp.

After six months of properly widening my jaw, I was finally ready for braces. I was happy I could feel the roof of my mouth again, but I hated the layer of metal that masked my teeth. I dreaded the monthly appointments where I had to get my wires upgraded and tightened. The orthodontist's office was a trek from our house, which gave me ample time to bitch and moan to my mom on the ride home. My teeth hurt. The edge of the wire was cutting into my cheeks. I was in agony.

"*Bemeeram barat*," my mom would say. "I'll die for you." It's what Persian parents frequently say to their kids when they voice even the slightest discomfort.

"I'm tired."

"I'll die for you."

"I'm hungry."

"I'll die for you."

"I'm bloated."

"I'll die for you."

"*Khoda nakoneh*," I'd mumble in reply. "God forbid."

My braces came off during my sophomore year of high school. By then, I was consumed with other insecurities: bad skin, a boyish physique, a stereotypically large Iranian nose. There wasn't much I liked about myself. But for once, I was giddy as my mom drove us home from my appointment. I kept gliding my tongue along my teeth, stunned by the sensation. And I couldn't stop smiling at myself in the car visor mirror.

My parents and all my friends agreed: my teeth were *perfect*.

"Thank you," I finally told my parents.

But as my dad proudly smiled back at me, my joy was quickly replaced with guilt.

One day, I told myself, *I'll be successful, I'll have a lot of money, and I'll return the favor.*

Three weeks later, I was in the throes of every teenager's worst nightmare: I'd lost my retainer. I'd wrapped it in a paper towel during a meal and accidentally thrown it away. I frantically dug through the trash in our backyard, praying to the universe that I would find it. I never did. My parents would have to spend a few hundred dollars to replace it to keep my perfect teeth intact. I hated myself for being so irresponsible. This time, tears accompanied the guilt.

For most children of immigrants, guilt is a familiar emotion. Hell, it's more like a state of being. We don't require verbal reminders of our parents' sacrifices. We bear witness to them every day. We can see it on their tired faces when they come home from a job that pays the bills but wasn't what they'd dreamed of doing with their lives. We can see it in the faraway look in their eyes when they wax nostalgic about a country they loved but had to leave. We can see it when they sheepishly ask us to proofread something they've written for grammatical or spelling errors, when they fumble or get embarrassed because the person on the other end of the phone can't understand what they're saying. All parenting requires some form of sacrifice, but not all

AT THIRTY-SEVEN, I STILL FEEL PANGS OF GUILT WHEN SOMEONE COMPLIMENTS MY STRAIGHT TEETH.

parents choose a lifetime of feeling marginalized so their children can flourish and bask in the freedoms they were denied.

It would take more than twenty grueling years for our family to become American citizens. My parents were relieved when our immigration ordeal was finally over, but that doesn't mean they live in a country that makes them *feel* American.

A few years ago, my mom and dad downsized their lives, sold their house in Silicon Valley, and purchased a condo in the less expensive town of Brisbane, California. They can't afford to retire, but they've finally been able to put some money away.

At seventy years old, my dad got his teeth fixed. I never did make good on the promise I had made to myself. He covered all his own dental bills. His smile is beautiful now, but it was beautiful then, too. It was, after all, the marker of my happy childhood.

At thirty-seven, I still feel pangs of guilt when someone compliments my straight teeth.

"I had braces," I always explain.

But there's more to the story. My teeth, my *smile*, are evidence of immigrant parents, who would do anything for me.

This piece was previously published on LennyLetter.com.

FLOCK BY KELLY BASTOW

NOT BY THE HAIR ON MY CHINNY CHIN CHIN

BY KELLY JENSEN

I stare at my face more than the average person does.

Or rather, I stare at my chin more than the average person likely even thinks about theirs. It's not that it's too round or too square, too sharp or too soft. My chin is perfectly suited for my face and for my body.

I stare at it because it's peppered with sharp black hairs every single day.

Whereas many cis women don't deal with a secondary sex characteristic typical of cis men, I'm one of the lucky ones who wake up each morning with a need to pull out their sharpest tweezers and stand in the most well-lit bathroom in the house to spend upward of half an hour pulling out the stubborn hairs. Going hair by hair, the process is exhausting on my hands, which cramp up from such precise plucking. I've made my way through more than one pair of the best tweezers on earth because the idea of sending my tweezers in for a sharpening and being left without a pair to use on the daily—or worse, having to wait upward of two to three weeks to get them back—isn't something I can imagine. I too-regularly think about a meme that pops up periodically on social media about how if a girl is in the hospital, her bestie will show up and pluck that one annoying chin hair before anyone else notices, and I feel a tingling sensation, wondering how anyone would have the patience to do that for me.

Or worse, how I could trust anyone to even know I needed to do this much work to keep my chin stubble-free.

It began in college. My body began rounding out more and more, the bulk of my weight resting right in my middle. I'd always been fat; pictures of the women on my mom's side of the family showcase the same stocky body type generation after generation. We have German bodies made for working in fields, hauling goods, and carrying babies. Add to that the Sicilian heritage on my dad's side, and my body was, from the beginning, meant to be bigger than average.

But it wasn't a freshman fifteen I gained. Nor was it a freshman twenty or thirty. It was a freshman fifty, followed over the next few years by roughly fifty more pounds, which stuck to my body.

Along with the added weight and new first digit on my clothing size, my skin continued to be riddled with acne. I'd always had rough, zit-prone skin, but I'd been promised again and again that it'd get better as I got older.

But it didn't. It only got worse, and after I tried out several medications before college and didn't see any positive results, it felt pointless to try again. Bad skin was my destiny, and though it was annoying, I'd acquired enough skill at covering it up with makeup that I knew I could eventually learn to live with it.

Then there was the hair.

It began slowly. A rogue chin hair or two would pop up once a week or so, and it wasn't hard to get rid of them. I even made a joke to a high school friend one night online that I'd gotten my first chin hair, meaning that I was now officially "old." We laughed about it, exchanging weird body experiences that we'd each had, and chalked them up to "just getting old!"

By senior year of college, though, things took a decidedly unfunny turn. Though I lived with a roommate and had a long-term boyfriend, I feared what would happen if I had to travel or fell asleep in a friend's room one night. The chin hair had become not a weekly challenge, but a daily one. I'd sometimes come back to my room at two or three in the morning after a long night editing the school's newspaper and turn on the desk lamp, which emitted the perfect amount of unnatural light to show me just how bad the trail of hair had grown in the last twenty-four hours. I'd pluck until they were all gone, leaving my tweezers in the same cup as my pens and highlighters. It was a key tool, as much as the writing utensils, in my daily arsenal.

I convinced myself the hair was obvious. Minutes of plucking turned into tens of minutes, and never once did I consider that I should get it checked out. *My mom had chin hairs*, I told myself, *and there's nothing wrong with her.* If it was something I should worry about, I believed she or anyone else who was very clearly noticing this about me would say something.

No one did.

Plucking my chin hair became as routine as things like brushing my teeth. I did it because it was part of the routine. Except not only did I never talk about it, but I put off seeking help for it. And worse, I began fearing what would happen if anyone found out. Anxiety clawed at me whenever I was invited to stay somewhere overnight, which might mean spending time with someone in the morning before I could get in the bathroom and pluck. I checked the websites of hotels I'd be sharing with other people, making sure the bathroom had a sink and a mirror behind a door, rather than out in the open. If I couldn't figure it out beforehand, the bathroom check was the first thing I'd do when walking into a room. And if it was one of those setups where there was a door separating the sink area from the shower area, I'd set my alarm so I could wake up much earlier than any of my roommates so they wouldn't notice how long I spent behind the locked door and think it was weird.

Keeping up this routine was exhausting on every level. I also knew that continuing to pretend the problem didn't exist was, in fact, a significant part of the problem.

On a routine visit to my doctor, after she'd done a breast and pelvic exam, I said something.

She sat back in her chair and listened to me talk about all the things I'd been documenting over the last ten years. The weight I'd gained—some of which had been lost through both healthy and unhealthy means, but which was, ultimately, something I'd come to accept as part of who I was—nonstop acne, a painful and embarrassing recurring boil at the root of my breast, and finally, the part that was hardest to choke out: the hair.

I had done my research over the years because, despite not wanting to know, I desperately wanted to know. I'd found forums and web pages dedicated to people who had many similar physical symptoms. Within those forums, I'd found cis women who, unlike me, had allowed their chin hairs to grow out, not caring at all what other people might think. I remember a late-night search led me to a woman who not only let the hair grow out but dyed it funky colors, carrying pride in something that—for me—was a trait to be ashamed of. What all those searches amounted to was a potential diagnosis of polycystic ovarian syndrome (PCOS). I asked my doctor what she thought, and she sat with me in that office for far longer than most doctors would, poring over guides and diagnostic tools she had on hand. She agreed it sounded quite like what I'd described, and she wrote me a referral to a specialist in women's reproductive issues to get a diagnosis that she wasn't qualified to give.

PLUCKING MY CHIN HAIR BECAME AS ROUTINE AS THINGS LIKE BRUSHING MY TEETH.

The postdiagnosis years could be described in only one word: maddening. The thing about PCOS is that it's not a condition one can readily diagnose. It's a collection of symptoms that are lumped together as a diagnosis after all other possible avenues are traversed. This meant I gave a lot of blood, a lot of time, and a lot of tears to come to a *potential* conclusion about the chin hair, weight gain, irregular menstrual cycle, and acne. I wasn't diabetic. I wasn't struggling with a thyroid condition. I didn't have X or Y or Z. I didn't even have ovarian cysts—which, despite the condition's name, a person doesn't need to have in order to be diagnosed with PCOS. PCOS itself isn't a reproductive issue, either. It's an endocrine disorder.

More frustratingly, there's no cure. Despite the fact one in ten people with uteri have PCOS, there's infuriatingly little research for a cure or even a way to solidly diagnose the issue. Instead, the symptoms are simply managed, one by one.

My doctor suggested birth control. She said I'd see my skin clear up and it was possible the chin hair would become less noticeable. It worked for my skin, but did nothing for the hair. I stuck with the pills, though, because for the first time in my life, my skin was clear.

But with gorgeously clear skin came a new discovery: the chin hair became *more* obvious on my pale white skin. Or, at least, it became more obvious to me.

I spent a few days with a friend in her tiny city apartment, and with the tiny apartment came a tiny bathroom. This bathroom had no windows, and the only light was a buttery yellow overhead. No matter how many ways I maneuvered myself in there, I could not make out what my chin hairs looked like.

That morning I did what I'd never done before: I told someone about this struggle and how frustrating it was.

Her kitchen window had beautiful light, and it overlooked an empty courtyard. I took my hand mirror and tweezers out and sat on the sill. She grabbed a seat at the table as I began the plucking process, one hair at a time, my chin tilted toward the world outside. I told her how annoying this routine was and that my chin hair caused the weirdest, deepest sense of shame about my body. I didn't care about the acne. I didn't care about being fat—I embraced that. The fact that I was missing one of my front teeth was more of a fun fact than something to be ashamed of—that you couldn't tell, thanks to modern orthodontics, certainly didn't hurt. I'd stopped shaving my legs that year, wearing shorts and skirts more frequently than I ever had before, not caring if someone was turned off by my not conforming to societal expectations for women's hairless legs. It was too much work for too little reward.

It was the chin hair that made me feel embarrassed and ashamed and worried about what people might think of me.

I would never have known if you didn't say something just now, my friend said to me. *Both about the hair and the worry.*

Her voice was sincere, and I knew she wasn't lying, because she never once turned to watch me as I performed my tweezer ritual. We didn't go deeper into that conversation, but the next morning, I spent a little less time plucking my hair at her kitchen window, and the day after, even less time still.

It took another year for me to tell my doctor I wanted to get off the birth control. For all it was doing to help my skin look great, the hormones in the pills made me less well in other parts of my physical and mental health. I swung from mood to mood between breaths and struggled with painful headaches and cramps prior to my period; these were things I'd never experienced before toying with my body's natural hormonal composition. While forgoing birth control isn't an option for all who struggle with PCOS, it was an option for me, and it was one I realized I needed to take. The symptom-by-symptom method of managing the illness was too much work and made the things about my body that functioned fine do exactly the opposite.

My skin is still clear, and my chin hair still grows in every day.

I regularly think about the woman who dyed her chin hairs. The picture she shared on that forum I found nearly ten years before showed a close-up of the green hairs, which had grown out from prickly shards to softer, baby-fine strands. She noted how hard it was at first to make peace with this part of herself, but when she did, she realized that if people were going to stare, she would make it worth their while—and hers. She wondered if someday her chin hair would be long enough for her to make tiny little braids.

I'm not that comfortable with my own chin hair, and I'm not sure I'll ever stop thinking about the sharp black hairs that poke up every day. But what I have done is stopped making preparations for my daily ritual and stopped worrying about how my face might look in the morning.

Instead, I look myself in the mirror every day. I pay attention to my eyes, noticing when they're more blue than their normal green. To my eyebrows and how I'd like to shape them. To my lips and the Cupid's bow made to rock red lipstick. To the spray of freckles across my skin and the larger ones that stand out. To the way my jaw changes shape depending upon the time of the month and how hydrated I am. To the pink flush on my cheeks, if I've spent any time outside in the sun recently.

If someone wants to stare at the chin hairs I missed or skipped or ignored, I can only hope that they're staring at those things, too.

They *all* help to make up who I am.

How and why do tattoos stay on our skin?

Whether or not you have or want a tattoo, the mechanics behind them are fascinating. Tattoos, done either by machine or by hand, are made by needles that pierce the epidermis (the outer layer of skin). The epidermis is constantly shedding and is replaced by more skin cells from deeper within that layer.

Tattoo needles enter the second skin layer, called the dermis. This layer of skin contains things like your blood vessels, hair follicles, and glands. Because tattoo needles damage the dermis, the body responds by sending white blood cells to heal the wound. But since the ink pigment is too big to be absorbed by the white blood cells, it stays on that layer of skin permanently. This means that it becomes a part of your skin, and it's subject to the same sorts of things your skin is: stretching, shrinking, wrinkling, and more.

Removing tattoos is possible, though it's far more challenging than getting one. Removal involves a laser that homes in on a single pigment and breaks it up; this allows white blood cells to perform their normal duty of flushing out foreign elements from the body. It might take several treatment sessions to rid the body of all the ink pigment, and even after several sessions, the tattoo may not be removed entirely.

BODY TALK

FAQS

VISIBLE SCAR CLUB

BY D. M. MOEHRLE

~~~~~

1. Adults are too polite. Kids, still growing their sense of what the world is supposed to look like, notice any deviation. They always ask, What happened to you? What happened to your face?

When I was a kid, other kids asked me this relentlessly. We moved over and over again throughout my childhood, so I got to answer the question on every new playground, in every new cafeteria. To be scarred on your face is to be visibly and irrevocably separated from the norm in a way that is impossible to hide and that draws eyes in—or, at least, that's how I have felt.

The strangest feeling is when someone doesn't ask directly—when I hear, somewhere behind me, a small voice asking, "What happened to her face?"

2. "Do you want to know," the Joker asks, "how I got my scars?"

3. Now that I'm an adult, my friends tell me the scars are hardly visible. But that is not what bothers me. What I struggle with is that even though people say they don't notice, *I* notice my difference every day in every reflective surface. There isn't a day that passes when I don't look, pause, feel grotesque, feel alone, feel invisible, or feel *something* regarding my facial scars. The human eye always seeks out what is different. My eyes see the marks on my face where I was mauled by a dog before I was old enough to remember.

It's not what people like to hear. They want a story of survival and preternatural bravery. They want anyone who has such a visible indicator of their past to be a poster child.

4. In movies and books, scars denote men who are villains and women who are victims. Sometimes writers flip the script—the tragic male hero with his "horrible" scars, the evil female character whose scars indicate her untrustworthiness. In 2017's *Wonder Woman*, the female-led superhero movie I'd been waiting years for, the villain is Dr. Isabel Maru, also known as Dr. Poison. She wears a half mask to cover what we later see are significant scars on her jaw. In interviews, the actress who played Dr. Maru, Elena Anaya, spoke of the possibility that her character's injuries were a result of self-experimentation. In the middle of a movie apparently about female empowerment, one of the villains is a woman defined by her disfigurement. Her scars are shorthand for her evil.

5. The older I get, the less comfortable I feel speaking in absolutes. Saying things like "Everyone wants to be beautiful." I have no right to speak for everyone. Similarly, I can't speak for everyone with a facial difference. What I know is that beauty is particularly prized in our society and that those of us with facial differences rarely meet the criteria for beauty.

I felt bad when I was a teen and realized that I would never be a model, not due to height (though I am short!) or body type (though I'm not thin enough to be a traditional model!), but because of my face. Never mind that I didn't aspire to be a model. The inability to choose that career path if I'd wanted to made me sad. I wanted all the choices to be mine, and I didn't want a choice removed because of something that had happened to me, something I couldn't help. Believe me, I know how that sounds.

The teasing and the staring never got to me. The lack of choice left me wondering what might have happened, if only.

6. And then there are the objects of pity. In books like *Wonder*, written by a woman without a facial difference who was inspired by her son gawking at a stranger (a book that later became a movie starring an actor with no facial difference in a large amount of prosthetics), the person with the facial difference doesn't matter except in terms of what they might represent to the "normal." The poster child. These pieces of entertainment ask us, Isn't it brave to be alive while looking so grotesque? Don't the disfigured have so much to teach us after all?

Mask was the movie of my era, a grittier and more realistic story about a real boy named Rocky Dennis, whose face was distorted by a rare condition. *Mask*, with a bravura performance from Cher as Rocky's drug-addicted, biker-gang-member mother, shied away from the after-school-special stereotypes but still tried to convey the same messages as all the other inspirational movies about people "overcoming" differences: don't judge people on their appearance, people with disabilities are inspirational, and everyone should aspire to live in the moment.

Mine is not a story of inspiration. I'm not here to make people feel better about themselves. I don't live in the moment. I'm just getting through life, like everyone else.

7. It's easy for me to go about my day as a supposedly average person. I enjoy privileges as a cis white woman, and aside from the scars, I have no visible disability. Still, I instinctively look at the camera with my "good side." Or I put my chin in my hand to cover the scar on my jaw. I want to be unmarked. I want to forget.

A desire to be beautiful is what makes us diet, wear makeup, get surgery, hide away, expose ourselves. We work at the business of beauty.

We try our hardest. We want to look in the mirror and see the version of ourselves that will stop traffic, stop time, stop the feeling that we aren't good enough from welling up inside. But in most cases it seems like beauty isn't a choice. People are born with certain features, and some features go in and out of fashion. Things can be accentuated, exaggerated. But the widest range of us are just—average. It's what makes us hunger to look at beauty and want it so badly for ourselves. I feel locked out from being truly beautiful, and that makes me feel both ridiculous and incredibly human.

8. The opening sequence of *Mommie Dearest*, a film that is a cult classic, a camp masterpiece, a horror-drama, and a tragedy all in one, shows us Faye Dunaway as Joan Crawford torturing herself for beauty. She scrubs her face with boiling water, then plunges it into a bowl of ice. She applies creams and serums. Throughout the film, Joan is haunted by the awareness that she is growing older and, in her mind, less attractive. Without her beauty, who is she? Just a child abuser who can't force the world to conform to her need for control and order. Without our looks, do we have anything to offer the world? Joan didn't think so, and she grew more and more angry and twisted as a result.

We all have ugliness inside us—that much I'm comfortable saying as an absolute. Envy, pride, anger. We've been trained by the media to expect people's exteriors to reflect their interiors, but in real life they rarely do. If you looked at the scars on my face and pegged me as a comic book villain, you'd be wrong—I don't have any plans to destroy Gotham.

9. Here's something inspirational: it turns out most people are too wrapped up in themselves to notice you. My friend with a facial port-wine stain would often try to cover it with makeup, until they gradually

IT TURNS OUT MOST PEOPLE ARE TOO WRAPPED UP IN THEMSELVES TO NOTICE YOU.

realized few people noticed it in the first place. When the Joker takes off his makeup and disguises himself as a policeman in *The Dark Knight*, no one recognizes him despite the visible scars on either side of his mouth. At a certain point, the kind of person who will stare at your differences is the same kind of person who stares at wheelchairs and crutches, babies having too much fun, elderly people moving slowly, and anything else they deem outside the norm—as if that weren't subjective, as if they define what is and isn't right in the world.

10. These days, when a child stares at me, when I hear the faint "What happened to her face," I ignore the embarrassed parent, look directly at the child, and tell them I was bitten by a dog as a kid, but I'm OK now.

I can see them digesting this information, taking in a new fact about the world and putting it in their brain for later. I can't tell them to be kinder or to be unafraid or to react a certain way when they see visible differences; I can only let them see me and my normalcy, and hope they take that out into the world with them.

Marked at Birth

LIBBY VANDERPLOEG

I was born in 1978, a happy, healthy baby, with a big ol' rosey birthmark on my chest.

Most of my early childhood, I can't remember anyone mentioning it, so I didn't think much of it either!

WHAT'S THAT?

WHAT? MY BIRTH-MARK?

But of course, kids are obsessed with differences and as I grew up, I got more and more questions about the big, pink splotch on my chest.

People always asked...

IS THAT A RASH?

DID YOU GET HIT?

... or ...

IS THAT A HICKEY?

C'mon, obviously not! It's like 4" across.

MOM, WHAT'S A HICKEY?

WHERE'D YOU HEAR THAT?!

By my late teens, I was super over people asking me about my birthmark. I didn't need girls telling me that they didn't even notice it, or guys reassuring me that they actually thought it was kinda hot. Why?!

On the contrary, my grandma suggested I get it removed, presumably so I could be more normal.

Yeah, I'll admit, she got to me a little. But then I realized how little I even cared about that birthmark! I hardly ever noticed it.

I was 18 or so then, now 40 years old, and while I wouldn't have chosen this birthmark, I think I might finally kind of love it. I'm old enough that people don't really ask about it, and it's actually kind of fun to show it off without explanation. In fact, I even bought a pair of rosey trousers to bring out its color!

MARKED AT BIRTH BY LIBBY VANDERPLOEG

COSMIC FORMS

YOU'VE LIKELY HEARD THE TERMS *BODY POSITIVITY* AND *FAT POSITIVITY*.

You've also likely heard how important it is to love your body, no matter the shape or size. But hearing these things and believing them are different. It can be confusing and downright challenging, especially because our culture prizes a specific set of (often unattainable) race- and gender-specific physical attributes.

There is certainly value in loving your body. And there is absolutely value in discussing, expressing, and celebrating your body shape and size. But getting to the point of accepting your body as it is takes work, and some days it's easier than others.

This section digs deep into the various shapes a body can take, as well as what it means to grapple with contradicting emotions and messages about loving—or not loving—what your body looks like.

FIFTY SWIMSUITS

BY JULIE MURPHY

~~~

Fat people love being in water.[1] It's science.

OK, well, you shouldn't actually quote me on that. But I can say with absolute certainty that every single fat person I know loves swimming and being in the water. The social aspects of going swimming, however, can be a totally different story.

Having been a fat kid, I fondly remember the magical time in my life when I was too young to care about what I looked like in a swimsuit. I spent countless hours in pools, running through sprinklers, and even splashing around in a refreshing summer rain in my swimsuit.

Anything that could potentially involve water was top priority for this little chunky girl. I wasn't concerned with how I had to wiggle around to get swimsuits over my tummy or how the selection of swimsuits for bigger girls was limited in color and design. I only cared that I could get my tush down the Slip 'N Slide or could cannonball into the deep end with the rest of them.

And then something happened. My sister grew out of her leopard-print rainbow swimsuit and passed it down to me. To my four- or five-year-old eyes, this was a sacred moment. I'd coveted this particular swimsuit for years, and finally, the leopard-print rainbow torch would be passed on to me. It was the coolest swimsuit I'd ever owned, and I was in love. I felt like a freaking Olsen

---

1 I often say I was always the tallest, fattest, loudest person in every classroom growing up. I very deliberately use the word *fat* for a few reasons, but mostly because it was weaponized against me for so long, and there's power in words, so why not take back that power? If I just stopped living in fear of being called fat, then anyone who might use that word to hurt me would have no power over me. So anytime I talk about my body, I like to make it clear that I use the word *fat* and I use it on purpose. If the word *fat* offends you, I'm sorry. But I do hope you'll consider doing the emotional and mental work it takes to reframe that word.

twin. For the first time in my life, I felt cool and maybe even a little bit dangerous. I felt elegant too, like a ballerina or a gymnast. I pranced around our house in that swimsuit year-round until the day I outgrew it, which came way too soon.

As my body became drastically different from those of my peers, I quickly turned into the girl who showed up at pool parties and "forgot" to bring her swimsuit. Friends' moms would offer to loan me something of theirs or shorts and T-shirts belonging to dads or older brothers, but not only was I unable to bring myself to get into a pool in front of other people, I also could not admit why that was. If I told my friends I was scared of them seeing my body, they might know I was fat, and if they knew I was fat, they'd all reject me forever, right? (What is it about clothing that makes us think no one could possibly imagine what's hiding underneath? Trust me. No one who has ever interacted with me in my entire life has looked at me and thought, *Hmm, I bet there's a thin woman hiding underneath that dress*. I know that now, of course, but hey, I never said logic was my strong suit throughout adolescence.) And so I spent much of middle school and high school (in Texas!) with my Lane Bryant jeans (which, I swear to God, came up to my boobs) rolled up to the knees and my feet in the pool while all my classmates and friends dived and splashed around me.

My swimsuit anxiety continued on into my early twenties, but a few times here and there I allowed myself the mercy of saying "Fuck it" and raced in and out of a pool before anyone could see my cottage cheese thighs. I wore T-shirts every once in a while, even though they weighed me down in the water and did nothing to hide my legs, the part of my body I was most ashamed of. I remember lying in bed as a teenager and praying for smooth legs. I could live with being fat if only I could have smooth legs, free of cellulite. That, I believed, would change everything. Like I'd have the perfect legs and suddenly my whole life would fall into place, because obviously the only thing standing between me and my wildest dreams were my chunky thighs.

Two things changed for me in my midtwenties: (1) I slowly realized that hating my body allowed the patriarchy to control me (I hated my body, but I hated authority even more), and (2) I began working for plus-size retailers and was inundated with fat bodies every day. FAT. PEOPLE. EVERYWHERE. Fat people on ad campaigns. Mannequins shaped like fat people. Fat people in fitting rooms, asking for help with zippers or bra measurements or opinions. Fat coworkers.

At first, I felt really disgusted by other fat people. I thought maybe I knew something they didn't. I knew the truth: that fatness was a temporary state, and any effort to try to make myself comfortable or—gasp!—happy was a Band-Aid on a very fat problem. I cringed at the sight of other people's rolls and bulges. But exposure therapy is real, y'all! And the more fat people I saw, the more normalized fat bodies became to me. Not just normalized, but glorified! Suddenly, I was finding fat people attractive and interesting and even enviable. Not only had the patriarchy taught me to despise my own body, but it had done so by putting only a very specific type of body on a pedestal: white and thin. Television, movies, magazines. They'd all sold me the same lie, and I'd bought into it for way too long.

I hesitate to say I've learned to love my body. Loving my body is a new challenge every day, and sometimes I succeed, while other times I don't. But since I've been making a conscious effort to love my body, I've had the great fortune of reintroducing myself to so many things I loved as a child that were taken from me as I grew up. Those things range from exercise to travel to selfies to food and beyond, but the thing that brings me some of my truest joy is purchasing swimwear.

It started with a gold-and-black leopard-print swimsuit that reminded me of my favorite childhood hand-me-down. I wore this swimsuit on my honeymoon to the Dominican Republic. At first, I was terrified to take my dress off as I stood on the beach with my partner (who thought I was super hot and still thinks so now). But as I looked around and saw a whole bunch of imperfect

people with wrinkles and rolls and even cellulite lying in the sun, I thought, *Why the hell
not?* I remember seeing pictures of myself in
that swimsuit after my honeymoon. My partner had brought an old film camera on the
trip, and without much warning, he snapped
a picture of me by the pool. No cover-up or
"flattering" pose. Just fat old me in a bang-
ing swimsuit. I was scared of the moment
he'd get the photos developed and I'd have
to see that picture, but when I finally did see
it, there was nothing to fear. I didn't think
I looked incredible or anything, but I was
happy and sun kissed and had sand in my hair. The girl in the picture didn't
care about what she looked like or what other people thought of her thighs.
She was just having a damn good time in a cute swimsuit.

> **THE GIRL IN THE PICTURE DIDN'T CARE ABOUT WHAT SHE LOOKED LIKE. SHE WAS JUST HAVING A DAMN GOOD TIME IN A CUTE SWIMSUIT.**

After that, my swimsuit obsession snowballed. Bikinis began to take off
in the world of plus-size fashion—I lovingly refer to them as fatkinis—and I
soon became the proud owner of my very first bikini. I've had moments that
felt like big milestones—wearing a swimsuit in front of my in-laws or post-
ing a bikini picture online—but for me, it all comes back to two very special
leopard-print swimsuits.

For so long I hated trying on clothing for real, concrete reasons (like the
fact that I couldn't find anything in my size or anything that excited me) and
also for more nebulous reasons (like how women are conditioned to dread trying on clothing and being confronted with the reality of their size). And you
wanna know what? Sometimes after all the internal work and all the effort
I've gone through to find brands that work for me, it still sucks. It can still be
bullshit. So sure, every day is a struggle, and sometimes the fight to just say
"Fuck yeah, my body is awesome as it is!" feels like an incredibly impossible

uphill battle. But as of writing this piece, I can tell you that I own well over fifty pieces of swimwear and that I strut my fat ass into as many pools as I can, as often as I can.

That's an excessive amount of swimwear, I know, and some days I feel wasteful and even vain. My mother-in-law (who I love and adore) always comments that she never sees me wear the same swimsuit twice, and now it's a running joke. Of course, I have the privilege of being able to accrue that much, but I think it's also worth considering that, like many fat people, I've never before had the luxury of being so frivolous. Thin people take the luxury of frivolity for granted. They take it for granted that they can walk into nearly any store and find something that fits them. Despite my collection of swimwear, I still don't have that luxury. But one thing I have found in my mounds of swimwear is power. It's the same power a fat person feels when they post a picture of their face that exposes their double chin. It's the same power another fat person might feel in eating and enjoying whatever kind of food they want in public. Or what someone with cystic acne feels when they go out without makeup. Or what someone with scars feels when they proudly display them. Or what we feel when we embrace any number of things that sometimes make us want to curl up in a hole and hide from one another.

I know it sounds simple or maybe even ridiculous, but the greatest revelations of my life have come in the moments when I've learned to embrace the things society has tried to tell me I shouldn't. And a big part of that for me has been showing off my jiggly ass and dimpled thighs in an amazing swimsuit. So go put on a swimsuit, flip a middle finger to the patriarchy, and remind yourself that you're a work of art and any fabric that drapes your body is luck to do so. You are powerful.

MY BODY, MY FEELINGS

BY PATRICIA S. ELZIE

I was raised in a home that focused on academics. I was my brain, and my brain was me. I played sports here and there, but I was taught that being intelligent was the most important thing a person could be.

If I wasn't eating or drinking, I practically didn't know I had a body at all until I was in my twenties. Having this relationship (or lack thereof) with my body for a big chunk of my life made the concept of body positivity seem alien to me, a person who felt body-neutral. I started becoming aware of my body in my midtwenties, when I became sexually active. I still didn't have any appreciation for my body, as I thought of my physical self only in relation to others. I couldn't imagine loving my body or being satisfied with my body, because it still felt like something I was just stuck with. My body was neither great nor terrible to me. It was simply there.

I have a better relationship with my body than I did in my twenties for sure, but I also have a confession: sometimes I don't fully love it. I know I am not unique in this; however, the body positivity movement tells me that outside forces are the reason we don't always love our bodies. The diet industry, the beauty industry, white supremacy, ableism, transphobia, fatphobia, and so on. I completely agree. We did not come into this world hating our bodies. I've read the books, read the articles, and followed the hashtags, and academically, I get it. I understand.

Yet. It is one thing to comprehend something academically, but it is another to react to it emotionally. For example, we all know that no one lives forever. Not our family. Not our friends. Not our pets. Not us. This is something we all know as truth, but even armed with this information, when we lose a loved one, we still suffer the blow emotionally. We still feel. We still react. We still mourn. So while I know that any dissatisfaction I feel about my body is a result of external input, at the end of the day, that feeling is still real.

To further complicate things, many of the voices in the body positivity movement, though well intentioned, suffer from a lack of nuance and intersectionality. Sonya Renee Taylor, founder and radical executive officer of TheBodyIsNotAnApology.com, is a major exception to this statement. The work she is doing is phenomenal in its inclusiveness and breadth. Her voice, however, seems to be an anomaly in the sea of White feminist voices talking about fat positivity disguised as body positivity. I say it is "disguised as body positivity" because it is so often fat-centric.

I fully support people actively loving their full-figured bodies, but my body is so much more than just its fat. My body is naturally curly hair that is thought of as unprofessional, as evidenced by the too-frequent news articles about Black women getting fired because of their hairstyles and Black students getting suspended or, worse, actually having their hair cut or shaved by school officials. My body is brown skin and therefore more likely to be victimized by police brutality, which is proven by the disproportionate number of Black people killed by police. My body has mental illness and therefore relies on medication to tell my brain to stop the obsessive thoughts so that I may sleep and to make room for hope and joy in a brain that is sometimes hijacked by depression. My body is queer and therefore my body's relationship with my wife's body is sinful and unnatural each time another piece of anti-LGBTQ legislation pops up.

These are all reasons why I don't love how the modern body positivity movement puts the focus on positivity, or if not positivity, then acceptance. By shifting its focus from fighting against policing people's bodies to, instead, encouraging us to police our feelings, the movement excludes so many people. My wife is transgender. Before she started hormone replacement therapy, she struggled to exist in a body that did not feel like home—was I to tell her she just needed to accept her body as it was? Of course not. That's downright awful.

The body positivity movement imploring us to love our bodies as they are can also result in odd lines being drawn about body modification. We're often told plastic surgery is bad, but tattoos and piercings are anyone's choice. We're told to not color our gray hair, because it's not shameful to age, yet it's totally OK to dye our hair blue or pink. Why are these boundaries being drawn? Who do they benefit? Where does gender confirmation surgery fall? Wearing makeup? Styling our hair? Getting a prosthetic limb? These examples are all vastly different—and yet they are all ways of modifying our bodies.

It makes me think that body positivity in its current state isn't about bodies at all. That, instead, it's about how we feel about our bodies, how we feel about the bodies of others, and how others feel about our bodies. Isn't dictating how we *should* feel just another tool of oppression? Another way to have us shift our focus from all that we could be achieving to, instead, closely monitoring our feelings about our bodies? And then allowing those in power to maintain their power while we're distracted, wondering if we're loving our bodies enough and in the "right" ways?

Sometimes we don't love our bodies, and I'm fed up with being told by everyone from RuPaul to Brené Brown that our capacity to love others depends on our ability to love ourselves. I'm done with the messages that I *must* love my body to achieve some kind of completeness, freedom, or happiness.

I want to be clear: I am not against loving our bodies. I'm very much in support of loving our bodies, not only through emotions but also through actions. I support loving our bodies in ways that are revolutionary. But I also support *feeling* our feelings and acknowledging that our feelings are our own and that no one can invalidate them. It isn't sustainable to suppress our negative feelings with a weight of positivity.

The modern body positivity movement also puts up boundaries around our emotions, forcing us to decide which are acceptable and which are a product of society and capitalism. Recently, I found myself feeling guilt about my happiness after a small weight loss. It wasn't from a diet. It wasn't from exercise. I'd left a demoralizing work situation and dropped some of the weight I'd gained due to stress. I was happy to have lost it but then was immediately ashamed by that feeling. I'd failed at body positivity. On the flip side, I understand that for some people, such as those who have or are recovering from eating disorders, being happy about weight loss can be a slippery slope, and the rush of losing that weight can send them into a downward spiral. These are the reasons why the body positivity movement needs to expand beyond an all-or-nothing mentality. Life is never 100 percent of anything.

Some people may never love their bodies fully or partially or at every moment. But no one should feel additional shame from a movement purported to be about positivity. We are not weak or less-than because of our emotional experiences, just as people who reach a high level of body confidence, body acceptance, or body positivity are not more-than. So what now?

I don't always love my body or how my body is devalued in this society, but I am grateful for my body. Maybe that's where the positivity lies for those of us who feel left out of the movement, and maybe that's how we can find comfort in our relationships with our bodies. Perhaps we can practice body gratitude and make space for the positive, neutral, and negative feelings. For the highs, lows, and everything in between. No matter where we're at, maybe focusing on being grateful, knowing that the gratitude may shift from day to day, will help us feel more consistently at home in our bodies.

I AM GRATEFUL FOR MY BODY.

In her book *The Body Is Not an Apology*, Sonya Renee Taylor writes, "When we liberate ourselves from the expectation that we must have all things figured out, we enter a sanctuary of empathy." Perhaps this is how: by knowing none of us has this completely figured out and we are all learning together. We must be patient with ourselves on our journeys and with others on theirs.

I may never be truly, madly, deeply in love with my chubby midsection or my gray hairs, but I am grateful that this body allows me to hug, write, and laugh, which are all much more important to me.

Is it OK to use the word *fat*?

As with any label applied to a group, each individual within that group will have a different preference. But generally, *fat* is the acceptable, preferred term to describe someone who is outside the medically and culturally defined average weight or physical build.

Fat is—and is not—a complicated term. Too often, it's a word used to describe a feeling. Fat is not a feeling; it is a physical aspect of a body. *Fat* is also not an OK word to use to make someone feel bad, to use as an insult, or to use as a basis for discrimination. Fat is a thing a body can have, just like hair or fingernails or a nose. Some bodies have more fat than others.

Fat activists have reclaimed the word *fat*, and if someone self-identifies as fat, it's not only acceptable but also encouraged to use that same language to describe them. A person who describes themself as fat has elected not only to embrace the word but also to celebrate it.

BODY TALK

FAQS

FAT OUT LOUD

BY ALEX GINO

~~~

I was twenty-three years old the first time I said the word *fat* out loud. I had already discovered the concept of genderqueerness and embodied it. I had already graduated from college, ditched one career, and started another. I lived on my own, had a full-time job, and was on my first-ever solo vacation: two weeks in the Pacific Northwest. But I had never said the word *fat*. OK, maybe I had whispered it to myself in the dark, but I had never said it at full volume, and certainly never in front of someone else.

At least, I don't remember saying the word *fat*, and I do remember avoiding it more adamantly than I avoided butter. If I never tried butter, I could virtuously say I didn't like it, and I wouldn't end up getting fat because I liked it too much. If I never acknowledged that I was fat, it wouldn't matter to me and I couldn't feel shame about it.

As if my grandmother hadn't given me a book called *Teenage Fitness* for my twelfth birthday because "I could go either way": thin success or fat failure. As if I hadn't grown up watching my mom lose the same twenty pounds over and over, only to find them again like the cat who came back the very next day. As if my ex hadn't told me that part of the reason he was no longer attracted to me was that I had put on weight during a winter bout of depression.

Avoidance isn't how butter works, and it's not how shame works. Not knowing what butter tasted like didn't mean I wouldn't be fat, and not naming my shame didn't mean I wasn't filled with it. Shame lives in the shadows. I was fat and needed to be able to talk about my body. I deserved to be able to talk about my body. I didn't want to hate my body—I never had. But I had never heard of someone loving their fat body, and that meant I didn't really know it was an option, much less how to do it.

So there I was, visiting my good friend Beth in Seattle. She's about my build (if a little taller) and wanted to share something with me, something she had just been introduced to herself. She handed me a brightly colored book with the title *FAT!SO?* emblazoned on the cover, above a delighted and delightful blond woman, a cartoon representation of author Marilyn Wann. Beth showed me that if you flipped the pages, a tiny, round Marilyn in the corner shook her stuff. It was a book filled with funny pictures and snarky commentary, and it said "FUCK YOU!" to the ideas that had been implanted so deeply in my mind that I hadn't even known I wasn't born with them.

IT WAS A LIFE-ALTERING MOMENT TO HEAR THE WORD *FAT* AS AN HONEST DESCRIPTOR, NOT AN INSULT.

Beth and I took turns reading out loud to each other. She went first. It was a life-altering moment to sit in that sunny Seattle room and hear the word *fat* as an honest descriptor, not as an insult. Fat as a source of joy, maybe even something to be proud of. I felt full, seen, and solid, beneath our giggles at Marilyn's effervescent style.

And then it was my turn. I don't remember stumbling or whispering. Like the title of the book said, I was fat. So? Shame about my shame multiplied into shame armor. It felt important to read the word *fat* as though it weren't a big* deal, when, in fact, it was massive.*

I was three thousand miles from home. None of it counted, like ice cream you were allowed to eat on that weird carbs-for-one-hour-a-day diet I tried for that ex who told me I was a lot less attractive when I was slightly fatter. I could claim it wasn't really me saying the word *fat*, acknowledging its existence in the world, in my body. (Back then, I still thought about fat as something people have, rather than something people are.) I was simply reading what Wann had written, with no personal attachment to any of the ideas. I was just experimenting with being the kind of person who said things like *flabulous* and *chub rub* without a second thought.

We must have read fifty pages aloud, and at some point, I realized we wouldn't be able to read the entire book together. I couldn't put this all on Beth, Seattle, and Marilyn, anyway. I would have to take on my own empowerment of my fat self. And you'd better believe I have. I bought my own copy of the book and finished it back home in Philadelphia, reading out loud when it felt like I needed to hear the words more deeply. I learned to smile at my body in the mirror. I rubbed my belly. I stroked my sturdy, dimpled thighs. It took time and focus, but once I stopped avoiding my own avoidance of my body (a full*-time job), there was nowhere for the shame to hide.

Since my trip to Seattle, I have grown quite fond of the word *fat* and of fat bodies. I've made lots of incredible friends and acquaintances who love their bodies and mine, and love to celebrate them. Many of us are soft and squishy and give great hugs. Radically self-loving fat people are some of the most fun, caring, thoughtful, special people I know, and lots of us are amazing cooks who are happy to share our tables. That doesn't mean we don't have rough days when the world gets to us, but we have each other. In hard times, I have been buoyed* by my fat queer community.

I've also learned that mine is only one of a wide* range of bodies and that this body I always saw as having "excessive" fat is really rather middling. I remember looking at myself in a mirror during my first NOLOSE conference (a radically feminist, fat-positive, queer space) and feeling smaller than I had ever felt. Not with pride or shame or anything but the realization that my archetype for people had been skewed to the thin for so long that I had seen myself at the high end of the spectrum. At four feet ten and having been in the range of 150 to 180 pounds my entire adult life, I am nowhere near the high end of the spectrum.

To be clear, *FAT!SO?* is not a perfect book, and I'm thrilled more books—both fiction and nonfiction—that respect fat people are being published, especially those by Black people, Indigenous people, People of Color (BIPOC); disabled folk; poor people; LGBTQIA+ individuals; and people from other marginalized groups, and I hope there are many more to come. In particular, I can't recommend *The Body Is Not an Apology* by Sonya Renee Taylor highly enough.

But oh, the shame I shed that day in Seattle. Not all of it, not nearly. But I had a new word to try on for size.* Language is powerful. It can provide connection and validation. It can also cause hurt and shame. My shame of the word *fat* was a mirror of the shame of my own body that was so deep I couldn't even name it. Changing my reaction to the word *fat*, and embracing it, has been a vital part of loving my fat body. I'm grateful that there was a tool for me when I needed it, and I'm excited for books like the anthology you're reading right now. The more we share honestly about our bodies and listen to others talking honestly about theirs, the closer we get to self-love.

Diets don't work. (Check the science.)

You are amazing right now. (Without a single change.)

You can choose to love yourself for who you are. (Not despite it.)

Good luck. (You got this.)

*All puns intended.

THIN

IN CHINA, THE STANDARD FOR A WOMAN'S IDEAL BODY SHAPE IS EXTREMELY THIN.

5'5"

IDEAL WEIGHT: 120 lbs

A4: ← 8.27" →

IN 2016, A POPULAR CHINESE SOCIAL MEDIA MEME SUGGESTED THAT ANY WOMAN WHOSE WAIST EXCEEDED THE WIDTH OF A PIECE OF A4 PAPER WAS CONSIDERED "FAT."

I CAME IN AT 140 POUNDS WHEN I REACHED ADOLESCENCE. IN THE CULTURE I GREW UP IN, THIS "FATNESS" WAS RATHER UNFORGIVABLE.

UGH... AGAIN...

YOU'RE FAT, TOO? LET'S LOSE WEIGHT TOGETHER.

125 POUNDS

PHEW! ONLY 110 POUNDS.

I'M NOT EATING THIS MONTH.

PHYSICAL EXAM

AND THE ONLY ACCEPTABLE WAY TO BECOME THIN WAS TO STARVE, NOT EXERCISE.

THE FAMILY TABLE WAS FERTILE GROUND FOR FAT-SHAMING TAUNTS.

BOYS LIKE THIN GIRLS. YOU DON'T UNDERSTAND YET.

OH MY GOD, THAT'S ENOUGH.

CAN YOU STOP EATING??

HONESTLY I NEVER EAT MUCH...

LISTEN TO GRANDMA! DO YOU EVER SEE FAT CELEBRITIES ON TV? NO! MAYBE THIS CAN HELP YOU CHANGE YOUR MIND?

(This was untrue—many Chinese male politicians flaunted astounding beer bellies in public appearances.)

THIN BY YAO XIAO

WHEN I MOVED TO THE U.S. I FOUND THE CONVERSATION AROUND MY BODY LESS PERSONAL, BUT AS A NEW IMMIGRANT, I DID NOT HAVE MANY PERSONAL CONNECTIONS.

Shopping alone at T.J.Maxx

SHOES AND CLOTHES THAT FIT ME? AMAZING!

MA'AM, WE'RE CLOSING.

I WENT THROUGH A PHASE OF BEING LONELY AND VAIN. THE SHAME BEGAN TO LOOK LIKE SOMETHING I COULD LEAVE BEHIND.

WHEN I STARTED TO SEEK OUT MORE CONNECTIONS WITH CHINESE COMMUNITIES, HOWEVER, I WAS SHELL-SHOCKED BECAUSE MY INSECURITIES WOKE UP AND SURGED.

YOU HAVE A VERY AMERICAN BODY TYPE.

EVERYBODY IS STILL SO THIN.

I WAS SO SELF-CONSCIOUS, NOTICING IF I WAS THE BIGGEST PERSON IN THE GROUP. AND MORE OFTEN THAN NOT, I WAS.

ASIAN ELDERS SEEM TO JUST NEVER LET IT GO. I'VE MOSTLY FORGIVEN THEM, THOUGH.

MY, AREN'T YOU HUGE!

MEETING THIS SHAME FACE-TO-FACE AGAIN IS PART OF MY PATH TO RECONNECTING WITH MY CULTURE AND THE REALITY OF MY LIFE.

WHAT DOES IT MEAN TO BE A WOMAN WITH CHINESE ROOTS?

IT HAS NOT BEEN EASY TO BE PRESSURED TO ACHIEVE "PERFECTION."

I LEARNED TO BE DISAPPOINTED ABOUT MY BODY FIRST, THEN TO PRETEND TO BE INDIFFERENT.

AND NOW I AM LEARNING TO LOVE AND CARE FOR MY BODY.

I AM ALSO LEARNING WHAT THAT REALLY MEANS.

MY BODY MADE ME AN OUTCAST. LUCKILY THIS MEANS I DO NOT ACCEPT THE STATUS QUO.

MY BODY, A CRIME

BY MARS SEBASTIAN

My name is Marissa, but many thousands of people just call me Mars. I became a social media influencer after two hashtags I created (#BlackoutDay and #LoveforLeslieJ) went viral a few years back. It's not difficult to get a sense of who I am from a glance at my profiles. I'm a Gemini; I'm a woman. I am many things. I'm also fat, and I have had binge eating disorder for a decade.

This is my first very public admittance of that fact. I felt shame because I thought that eating disorders were just for skinny white girls and that my suffering meant I was just being weak, so I kept quiet. Years of enduring fatphobia and experiencing erasure from discussions of disordered eating, combined with the urge to maybe not feel so alone, are pushing me to speak now.

Here goes.

I don't remember the time before I was hyperaware of my body and how much space it took up. I was always a tall, chubby kid from a tall, chubby family. I remember being envious of my smaller friends by the time I was eight years old. I learned early on that the nature of who I was informed the way the world treated me. I felt the weight of the world's fatphobia, misogyny, anti-Blackness, and colorism before I even truly knew myself. In a society that prioritized and rewarded very narrow ideas of "beauty" and measured worthiness based on those constraints, I, a fat Black girl, didn't stand a chance. What people called "beautiful" didn't look like me. The images that were shown to me in stores, in magazines, and on television sold me the idea that thinness and whiteness were gold standards of beauty.

I know that I hated my body by the time I was ten.

Middle school was a hellscape. I got called "cow" a lot. Big b*tch. By high school, I despaired that I was not thin, light skinned, and "pretty" enough to secure what I'd been taught were measures of success for a teenage girl.

At fifteen, I was so weary of my peers' ridicule and the damaging messages I absorbed while just navigating the world as a bigger girl that by the time my father started watching my plates, my relationship with food had already soured. "That's a bit too much," he said to no one else in my family but me, the fat teenage girl in a fat family. How was that fair? With every person in my family being overweight, why was I singled out? How could he lecture me when his portions were at least double mine? Looking back, I realize he genuinely did it out of love and concern for my health. He was dealing with weight-related and genetic illnesses, and since I was his first child and only daughter, comments about my portions became a love language of sorts. Diet culture prevented us from learning how to talk about weight and health in ways that were helpful, productive, and safe. How could he have known better? My dad's intention aside, the casual monitoring of my portion sizes stung, and the habit of obsessing over what I ate stuck. Family meals started to taste like sawdust. My portions slowly grew bigger out of resentment, and I was already too far down a road I still have trouble navigating.

The first time a boy I liked complimented me, he told me he admired my "thunder thighs" and my breasts but joked in passing about my stomach. I learned that only parts of my body were "correct." Curvy girls were preferred, but "no, not like that." Another lesson came when my peers ridiculed a classmate bigger and darker than I was. I don't remember her name, but I remember the way her face contorted as she tried not to cry. I was too scared to speak up. Instead, I pledged I'd never be like her. I learned that no one stands up for girls like us.

My senior year of high school, I was cast as Maria in *West Side Story*. I was a talented and capable soprano, and with the encouragement of my teachers, I learned all of Maria's music and lines. Halfway into rehearsals, and close enough to the show that we'd begun preliminary measurements for costumes, my teachers suddenly changed their minds. Shocked and embarrassed, I watched as girls lighter skinned and thinner than I was became Maria. I, along with other dark chubby girls throughout the ensemble, was benched. My consolation prize was singing a solo midway through the show as a nameless character. Girls like me weren't leading ladies. No matter how talented I was, my look wasn't right. Fatness wasn't acceptable. My skin tone wasn't beautiful. The fact that I dared to exist and take up space as

"BEAUTIFUL" WAS UNATTAINABLE, AND I BECAME STUCK IN A LOOP OF COMPLETELY GIVING UP ON IT AND THEN DESPERATELY CHASING IT.

a tall, fat, darker Black teenage girl? I would never win. I'd never be the thin, lighter-skinned, popular girl adored by many for her grace, beauty, and charm and rewarded with popularity and a parade of suitors for being all the right things.

"Beautiful" was unattainable, and I became stuck in a loop of completely giving up on it and then desperately chasing it. I would eat way too much in one sitting out of stress and hopelessness and then starve myself later. To avoid comments like my father's, I did my best to avoid eating in front of people. "I'm not hungry" became a reflex, as ingrained as hunger itself. I learned to completely ignore when my body told me it was too full or starving. It was only when I couldn't bear the pain of overeating or the dizzy sickness of starvation that I relented and fell into the cycle again.

I was seventeen and a freshman at NYU when a doctor put a name to my suffering and obsession—binge eating disorder. With my diagnosis came overwhelming relief and the grim determination to get to a place where my eating disorder couldn't reach me. It had gripped me for so long, silenced me, and gnawed at my sense of self. I became the meals I skipped. I became the foods I ate in secret. I became my ever-climbing dress size. Weight gain was the last thing I wanted, but it happened. It's not a story that's particularly uncommon, but as a fat girl with an eating disorder and as a person who *gained* weight because of their disorder, I've felt unseen for years. Almost a decade after my diagnosis, I am heavier than I have ever been, and I'm still struggling to recover.

We hardly speak about fat girls having eating disorders, and we haven't made space for fat Black girls and women to be seen and supported without ridicule. Not only does the world largely regard fatness as something to be avoided, but fat Black women are ridiculed within our communities as sloppy and unattractive, are made mammies and caricatures due to anti-Blackness, or are fetishized for our Blackness and our bodies. It's additionally frustrating that the most far-reaching "body positivity" spaces continually center white women and lighter-skinned Women of Color, most of whom will also fit into constraints about what type of fat bodies are more acceptable than others.

I'm hoping to challenge these constraints and start a wave of healing by being open with my story. I'm still recovering; I'm still fighting against all the ways this world tells me I'm unworthy. The stress of existing as I am sometimes manifests as relapses. I'm still trying, though, because I'm angry, and I'm ready to end the abusive relationship I've been in with my body due to fatphobic and racist standards of beauty. I'm ready for fat girls and women to be free. I'm ready to be free.

To close, a note to the unseen:

Dear You,

I am you, and I am with you. I am with you when you avoid mirrors. I am with you when you cry. I am with you when fatphobia goes beyond just feeling unpretty. When it causes the world to value you and your opinions and your labor and your life less.

I am with you when you imagine the Thin and Happy™ you. A smaller girl who walks into any store she wants with confidence. Who never panics while looking for the plus section. Who eats in public without second or third thoughts.

I am with you when you wonder if you'll ever be sexy outside of being fetishized. I am with you when you shroud your body in clothes that don't flatter you because you can't afford to be plus sized *and* fashionable.

I am with you when your thin friends and family embarrass you, even when they mean well.

I am with you when you are in pain. When you overeat from the stress and strain and feel awful. When you skip meals. When you purge.

We are worthy of wellness. We are worthy of recovery. Your body, your struggle, is not a crime.

—Mars

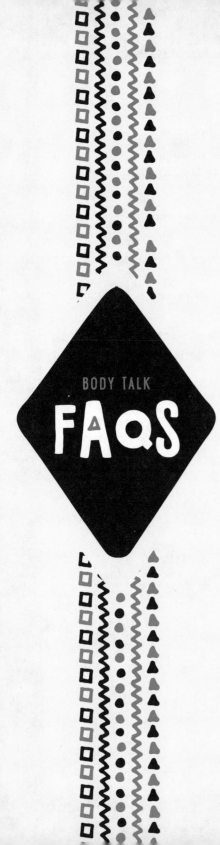

what's the difference between body positivity and fat acceptance?

Body positivity and fat acceptance can be seen as sister movements, but the way that each achieves its end goals differs.

The fat acceptance movement began in the 1960s. In the era that brought revolution to race, gender, feminism, and sexuality, fat activists also spoke up, advocating for the rights of fat people and revolting against size discrimination.

Where the fat acceptance movement was part of the radical shift in politics, the idea of body positivity became the more watered-down version. Over the last couple of decades in particular, body positivity has been based on the idea that all bodies are good bodies and that every person has something—or multiple somethings!—they're not especially happy about when it comes to their physique. Instead of focusing entirely on body size, it is based on the idea that there are countless ways our bodies can be judged. Body positivity includes fat bodies beneath its umbrella, but it often leaves out those with bodies outside an "acceptable" range and has instead focused on more media-friendly, average-sized bodies.

Body positivity has its benefits, though. For many, it's the first step in understanding how politicized our bodies can be. The body positivity movement can help people better understand the history of size discrimination and of how bodies became the target of capitalism, can lead to encounters with those who've been advocating for radical size acceptance, and may move more people toward taking part in fat acceptance.

NON-SKINNY PEOPLE WHO i THINK ARE SEXY AS HELL

by Tyra Banks

I like a bit of booty on my models, my missies, my matrons, and my men. I think these people are some fine-ass human beings.

ASHLEY GRAHAM: This statuesque supermodel stunner [was] also [an] *America's Next Top Model* judge and [is] my girl! She's the queen of the Curve-a-listas!

ZACH MIKO: The first supermodel to come out of Brawn, IMG's plus-size male model division. Chiseled, chunky, and oh so funky (and oh so fine as hell!).

CHRISTINA HENDRICKS: A redhead with curves so hot they could start fires.

KATE UPTON: My *Sports Illustrated* cover girl sister from another mister.

VINCE VAUGHN: 6'5" and looking good, boo. No beanpoles here.

AMBER ROSE: A beauty and a booty on a mission to stop slut shaming. I can definitely get behind that behind.

DASCHA POLANCO: Orange is the new black, and bootyful is the new beautiful.

The bearded man in the plaid shirt sitting next to me at this Malibu café right now as I type. (Damn, your thick lumbersexual ass is fine, boo!)

This piece was previously published in Perfect Is Boring *by Tyra Banks and Carolyn London.*

LOVING ON ME IS PRAYER: QUEER JOURNEYS INTO BLACK GIRL SELF-LOVE

BY JUNAUDA PETRUS-NASAH

"Junauda, are you ashamed of your body?" my mom asked me one morning. I was about twelve years old, getting ready for school, and we were in the bathroom of our small house. I was taking a bath in our claw-foot tub, lying on my stomach to hide my developing body from her opinionated eyes, and she was peeing. (Modesty or privacy was never an option in our home of Mama and her four daughters and one bathroom.) I told her I wasn't ashamed of my body, and I was lying. But I knew that was what she wanted to hear.

She saw right through my response and continued her inquiry.

"Junauda, you should love your body. I wish when I was your age that I knew how beautiful my body was." She spoke with a regret that made me pay attention. In that moment, I tried to imagine my mom as a girl like me, having feelings about her body. I was in the cooling bathwater, hiding the signs of my impending womanhood, while my mom, a Trinidadian woman with dark skin, striking features, and impenetrable self-esteem, even on this inglorious throne, implored me to see myself as stunning and complete. This moment, in all of its awkwardness, left me with a seed of insight: that I *should* love myself—love my body—even if it didn't seem possible then.

My mom didn't know what I was navigating in my middle school life. Every day in seventh grade in 1993 was like hood fashion police. *Deonte wearing the same pants as yesterday! Look who got on sneakers from Payless? Junauda got hair too nappy for relaxers, pink lotions, and hair gel! Who got high-waters on?*

Raphael try to be like Kris Kross but got tight-ass, high-water overalls that he wear backwards with one strap swinging and look busted? Who got socks with holes in it? Who in this classroom had sex before? Who smelling all musty and ain't put on deodorant? Who ain't matching? Got plaid and paisley on and faded hand-me-downs? Who got a hairstyle look like they in the third grade? These questions, posed by popular and grown-ass eighth graders during any given class—where were the teachers?—always stressed and panicked my young soul.

My clothes were always unremarkable, faded or hand-me-downs, and I had never kissed anyone (although I had an elaborate lie involving Raphael ready to spill if I was ever asked). I was always anxious I would be pulled into these interrogations. My family's economics and immigrantness and my awkwardness added to the challenge of me fitting in, so I stood out as one of the frequent targets. I had desires for boys in my school who would never see me as pretty, and I had desires for girls, too, something I was curious and simultaneously ashamed about and hid away from myself and the world. School sucked so bad sometimes, I would beg the hall monitor to let me sit in her office to avoid being teased for my hair and my nerdiness.

But in eighth grade I decided to stop trying to make my older sister's hand-me-down Girbaud and Cross Colours into an identity of a kid who wasn't poor, and instead, I started to dress grunge. I had been inspired by a White girl who was in band with me, who started skipping school and dyeing her blond hair a new color every week with Kool-Aid. She'd stopped caring what everybody thought, and somehow that seemed like the answer for me. To not care what folks thought and indulge in the path of the outsider.

By that time, Left Eye from TLC, Aaliyah, Björk, Claire Danes, and D'arcy Wretzky from the Smashing Pumpkins were among my style icons. I crushed on their androgyny and quirkiness, how they seemed to define their own kind of power and sexiness. All of them beautiful and irreverent, but also not quite like me. I listened to alternative music that reflected the Black-girl emo that hurricaned inside me, the one that no one seemed to care about. My mom was mortified when I would dress like I'd borrowed somebody's grandpa's favorite bingo outfit after he was attacked by piranhas. "You finish dress?" she would ask every time I would present my newest outfit. After I'd say yes, she would offer her opinion.

"Junauda, White children wear dem clothes, and people see it as a style. *You* wear dem clothes, they think your parents is poor, or we ain't care about you." The Caribbean-parent backlash was real. My mother couldn't understand why I would purposely try to look raggedy. Was this the American dream she had worked so hard for? But I loved how I looked. It felt powerful to look like I didn't care what anyone thought, even though I did deeply.

My eighth-grade year, my boobs were coming into formation. I was growing pubic hair and a thick ass, and every jerk on my block and at my school noticed and would holler some dumb and sexist insight to me about my body, which I was already devastatingly self-conscious about. In the early '90s the fashionable bodies were "36-24-36," a rare and sexualized ratio of bust to waist to booty. The other body type popular in media was so skinny that your hip bones and rib cage were visible, with no boobs or booty at all. Teen magazines, boys at school, men in my neighborhood, other girls at school, and the music videos I was watching, from hip-hop to grunge, all told me I had to have a specific body type to be lovable. This was also when I first learned about eating disorders, which seemed to me like a symbol of privileged-White-girl angst. They never felt relevant to me, even though shame and unhealthy habits, like eating sugar for comfort and extreme dieting, were settling into my psyche in insidious ways that would take years to release.

Brown and gap-toothed, I couldn't see the beauty in me.

By the time my mom had spoken to me while I was in the bathtub in seventh grade, I had already internalized messages about the value and beauty in my femmeness and Blackness. I have a vivid memory of ripping up my kindergarten school pictures when I was five because I thought I was so ugly. I was young, but I'd be lying if I said I didn't feel that way, with all my little heart. I had been playing with blond Barbie dolls, my dad had left my mom for a White woman, and those things, along with other messages I was getting about my Blackness from society and school, made me start to look at myself harshly. I was constantly in battle with my relaxed hair, which, despite the calming description of the process, burned my scalp, forcing my natural coils into brittle straightness. (I eventually went natural at fifteen, inspired by Lauryn Hill, and rocked a little Afro.) As a teenager, I hid in my hip-hop- and grunge-inspired uniforms of plaid button-ups, headwraps, and baggy jeans. This was a time in my life when I just wanted to disappear, and it seemed, instead, that more of me was appearing, growing, and maturing.

I COULDN'T SEE THE BEAUTY IN ME.

When my mom was fifteen, she became a mother for the first time. She was a little older than I was that morning in the bathtub. She would tell my sisters and me that she loved us and also that she hadn't been ready to be a mom when she became one. She would remind us that we could choose whatever we wanted for our future, that we were individuals, that our bodies belonged to us. In other ways she would also remind us that the world had ideas about who we were. Whether she was praising or critiquing us, there was always a harshly earned knowledge about what it meant to have a Black femme body in this world.

My heart and body were mine, and they also belonged to a line of women whose bodies were abused, overworked, sexually violated, and stigmatized for generations. Yet they still found pleasure in love, dancing, and expressing their beauty through intellect, movement, and adornment. My heart and body were mine, yet walking around as a teen girl felt vulnerable, scary, and depressing.

Over the years, my body has experienced my life with me and absorbed my feelings about myself. And I have underloved, disrespected, hated, disregarded, and harmed myself. I have starved myself for thinness and eaten until the point of vomiting when I was pushing down my feelings and anxiety. I have hated and critiqued my body and believed that was the right relationship to have with it. I have desired to contort into a form I believed would be more lovable to this world. I forgive myself every day for this and try my best to replace these feelings with sweetness today.

Healing is traveling back in time to meditate and love on the spirits of my younger selves and my ancestors. The selves who struggled with worthiness and violence so that I could love myself and accept the individuality of my existence and magic. I look at pictures of myself at different ages: five, nine, twelve, fifteen. I look at my selves, my Black and dreaming selves, and see the insecurity and doubt in my eyes. I speak lovingly with my younger selves and tell them they were always deserving of love, from myself and this world.

My body has been a sacred shape-shifter and a devoted temple to my beingness, and I haven't loved it as much as it deserves. It has danced until the sun came up and run from danger and fought for my sisters and me when I couldn't run. It has flung itself into the sky, submerged into deep oceanic waters, and tasted some of the most delicious meals the planet has to offer. My body has experienced pleasure and cruelty from lovers and myself. It has held my emotions, my undeniable and passionate truths, and the parts of me that need to be heard.

My body has been a vessel for those expressions.

These days I ground myself in meditations of love for my body, my face, my spirit, and my soul. I take time to look in the mirror and practice acceptance of myself. I look at my whole body and drink myself in slowly. I practice redirecting my spirit to loving on me. I seek to unlock portals of pleasure, peace, and insight that I deserve to experience on behalf of my ancestors. In these meditations I think about that seed of self-love my mom planted in me that early morning in the bathtub in the '90s. When I barely knew my body. Today, I smile to myself, grateful for her gift and the mantra to love on my body with unbelievable inquisitiveness and reverence.

BELOW THE BELT

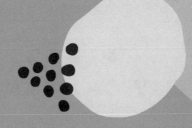

WHETHER OR NOT YOU CRINGE THINKING ABOUT WHAT'S GOING ON DOWN THERE,

it's important to talk about reproductive health. Whatever your gender, your genitals and reproductive organs can do things that are weird or uncomfortable, as well as awesome or pleasurable.

Sometimes menstruation can be painful enough that it impacts everyday living. Sometimes having testicles means that there's a chance of discovering a cancerous lump at a young age. Though we don't talk about these things enough, we should.

Let's get comfortable with being uncomfortable and talk about what's going on below the belt. These discussions can—and do—save lives, as well as offer compassion and connection for those who can too often feel alone when struggling with their own reproductive health.

PLEASE LAUGH: MY CANCER DIAGNOSIS

BY BENJAMIN PU

REASONS WHY I USED TO TOUCH MY NUTS

■ For fun ■ To check for cancer

I have testicular cancer.

Please laugh.

A few weeks ago, I went to my doctor for an annual physical exam. It went well. I had lost over twenty pounds since coming to the city (walking, eating right), my blood pressure was good, and my cholesterol was low. Then, we get to the part most guys are uncomfortable with. As it happens, the "turn your head and cough" joke is real life. But then my doctor paused. He found a lump.

He told me to see a radiologist as soon as possible.

Last week, I went to a midtown radiologist, had K-Y Jelly slathered all over my nether regions, and got an ultrasound by a very nice lady.

The results came back the same day. Cancer.

But not scary cancer. Ball cancer, the funniest of all the cancers.

Seminoma is the medical term for a neoplasm (new growth or tumor) that begins in, you guessed it, the testicles. Testicular cancer is the most common type of cancer for men between the ages of fifteen and thirty-five. It's easily treatable if caught early and has a 95 percent survival rate. So I'm good—I ain't gonna die because of no ball cancer.

The good news is that we may have caught it early. But we only caught it early because I went to the doctor.

I joked to my doctor that I touch my testicles all the time, and I didn't feel anything. I never paid attention to those PSAs about touching your junk to check for cancer. Cancer? Not me, I thought, so I'd rather touch my testicles for fun!

But unfortunately, it's all too real now. If it weren't for my doctor's medical expertise, I might not have known until it was too late.

If you have testicles but haven't gotten a physical exam in a while, or if you know someone who has testicles that has displayed a flagrant disregard for their medical health by not seeing a doctor recently, I have a message for you: **get your fuckin' nuts checked**.

Do your nuts have to be felt up by your doctor to find lumps or irregularities? No! In fact, the Testicular Cancer Society recommends that you do a self-exam every month. Feel yourself up in the shower. But do it properly, medically. I didn't do a monthly self-exam, and I may be paying some price for it.

As you may have noticed from the last few paragraphs, I'm taking this rather well. In fact, I'm joking about my diagnosis. Please don't be mopey around me, it makes me nervous. Frankly, I'm glad I can have such a positive attitude about this. Everyone copes in their own way, and I'm very happy that my natural instinct is to crack jokes and laugh at the phrase *ball cancer*.

Every single person I've confided in so far has the immediate reaction: "Oh no! Ben!" Which is a perfectly reasonable, normal reaction to have. And then they look sad. Which is why I immediately follow up with a joke about my balls. And that makes them feel better. And in a weird, fucked-up kind of way, it makes me feel better, too.

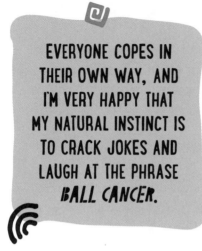

EVERYONE COPES IN THEIR OWN WAY, AND I'M VERY HAPPY THAT MY NATURAL INSTINCT IS TO CRACK JOKES AND LAUGH AT THE PHRASE *BALL CANCER*.

Still, am I scared? You bet I am.

This experience has been a whirlwind of firsts. I've never had a CT scan before; I have to go in tomorrow morning to check my lungs and lymph nodes. I've never thought about the possibility of not having children; I might have to freeze my future ones. I've never had so much blood drawn to run tests before. Also, I've never had cancer, so this is definitely a first.

I'll be honest, I'm having some trouble sleeping at night. I keep thinking about the operation I'll have to undergo (spoiler alert: it does not look like fun). I keep worrying about how much time I'll have to take off work. And I have to face the frightening possibility of undergoing chemotherapy and having my facial hair fall out. A tragedy!

But I'm a lucky one. The real tragedy would be someone else finding their cancer too late.

I'm making this public because:

1. Testicular cancer shouldn't be a taboo subject—after all, it is still cancer;
2. It's important for men to understand that testicular cancer is a very real possibility and you should get checked;
3. I'm an attention-grubbing loser. Give me a little slack, I have cancer!

If you're a man, touch yourself. If you know a man, get him to touch himself too. It might save his life.

And if you've got a great nut joke, please message me. I could always use a good laugh.

This piece was previously published on BenjaminPu.com.

KINDRED BY KELLY BASTOW

YOUR COMPLETE GUIDE TO SHANE'S SEX LIFE

BY SHANE BURCAW

Society has a disturbing infatuation with my sex life, and I'm not saying that in a Donald Trump "Everyone is so obsessed with me!" kind of way.

My blog has always had a feature that allows readers to anonymously ask me anything they want to know, and by far the most common questions are about my bedroom business affairs and the functions of my reproductive system.

Initially, it tickled me to respond to these questions publicly, because everyone seemed so impressed that "someone like me" could and did engage in sexual activity. I felt special, like a rare breed of the disabled population who had overcome the social stigmas surrounding disability to such an exceptional degree that I was worthy of sex. This, I later realized, was completely inaccurate, immature, and idiotic.

Sex and intimacy for people with physical disabilities is just as common and diverse as it is for any subpopulation of people. My desire to see myself as special or better than others in that sense was nothing more than a childish effort to bolster my insecurity-ridden ego.

Nonetheless, the general public's deep curiosity about my sexual abilities suggests there is an overwhelming lack of understanding regarding this issue. In an effort to clear up some of the confusion, here are a smattering of questions I've been asked by real people, as well as responses that I'm refreshing for the purposes of this book. Keep in mind, my experiences, shortcomings, methods, abilities, and inabilities are not meant to be representative of the disability community, the wheelchair-user community, or even the SMA community.[1]

And now that I've belabored the point long enough to guarantee I won't receive angry reviews for this chapter, I will begin.

People have asked me:

"Do you have a penis?"

Yes, six of them, actually. Every time one of my major muscle groups begins to weaken because of my disease, I grow an additional penis. It's an interesting—albeit rather useless—perk of spinal muscular atrophy.

"Can you get a boner?"

I can! They've been coming in heavy and healthy ever since puberty hit, and I guess even earlier than that, but prior to puberty I had no idea what they meant. When I was a little kid, I used to get them while lying facedown during physical therapy because of the way my groin pressed against the floor. That always made for an awkward surprise when the therapist rolled me onto my back for a new stretch. And that's a detail I've never shared with anyone until I wrote this book!

From what I understand, even though the penis contains muscles, the act of a boner rising to attention is more about blood rushing to that area of the body than muscle strength. My disease does not affect my blood flow.

"Do you masturbate?"

I wish I had kept a count of how many people have asked me this question through my blog. People question me about this so often that it's baffling. I try to imagine someone reading my blog—stories about breaking my femur, getting pneumonia, fearing death, going to the beach, etc.—and after all that information, the one thing they just need to know about me is if I fondle my own penis. Not that our lives are remotely comparable, but this feels akin to

---

1 Spinal muscular atrophy (SMA) is a neuromuscular disease that causes the progressive breakdown of motor neurons. There are several types, ranging in severity, but all forms of the disease cause progressive muscle weakness. —Ed.

reading a biography on Abraham Lincoln and coming away from the experience wondering only if he became constipated very often throughout his lifetime.

For all you perverts, I had the ability to masturbate until I was about eighteen years old. The trickier part of the whole process was the cleanup, which involved pretending my nose was running so that someone would give me a bunch of tissues. Throughout my teen years, I was plagued with a constantly running nose, or so it seemed.

When my arms and hands became too weak to continue this activity, my dignity took a hit. It felt like I was losing part of what made me a valuable man. I took solace in the fact that my penis worked, and that in the grand scheme of things, being able to jizz in a clump of tissues wasn't the most important ability.

"Can you/do you have sex?"

I can and I do, although my physical structure and ability requires some adaptation in the process. First, since I know my grandparents are reading this, I'll explain how my disease complicates standard, basic, run-of-the-mill sex, and then I'll share why I believe my disability actually improves sex and intimacy for my girlfriend and me.

As I've already established, my dick itself works phenomenally. The complications, then, are related to my muscle contractures. My body is stuck in a pretty rigid shape. When you don't use your muscles, they shrink, and eventually they become permanently tight. When I lie on my back, my body remains frozen in the sitting position, like a capital L tipped on its side. To imagine this, lie on your back and pull your heels up until they touch your butt. Perfect, now you're me!

The fact of the matter is that having sex requires certain parts of the body to be very close to each other, and when one of the participants is a crumpled mess of atrophied rigidness, that closeness can be tough to achieve. My partner can't simply hop on top of me, because if she did, my legs would smash into smithereens, and I suspect that would take some of the pleasure out of the experience.

Making love, then, becomes about finding positions that work. This often involves lots of bending, twisting, and contorting, which is why I only date gymnasts. My girlfriend and I have found some methods that work for us, and while we might look like a pair of grappling spiders, all that matters is that we're both enjoying the experience.

Early on it tortured me that I couldn't be a "better" sexual partner. My head was filled with damaging ideas about the importance of a man being able to perform in bed, and at times in my life, I was convinced that no woman in her right mind would ever want to be intimate with me. But as I became older and more experienced, I began to realize that intimacy in a relationship is so much more about the emotional connection than the physical one. SMA actually strengthens that aspect of my relationship. Having fun together physically requires us to communicate and listen to each other, which in turn makes us both much more aware of the other's pleasure. We've discovered that using our hands and mouths (and toes) is just as much fun as The Sacred Act. Once I abandoned the idea that sex needs to conform to society's narrow and ignorant guidelines—man dazzles woman by how hard and strong and fast he can gyrate his hips into hers—my sex life became much healthier and more enjoyable.

"Can you have children? Will they inherit your disease?"

Spinal muscular atrophy is a genetically transmitted disease, so there is a chance that any Shane Juniors I create will have the disease, but the likelihood of that happening depends on whether or not the mother of my kids is herself a "carrier" of the disease. One in forty people carries the genetic mutation that causes SMA. My parents, although they don't have the disease, are each carriers, which meant there was a one-in-four chance their kids would get it. It gets real science-y if you want to know more about it than that.

My plan is to have enough children with SMA so that our family outings look like some sort of day program for people with disabilities.

This piece was previously published in Strangers Assume My Girlfriend Is My Nurse *by Shane Burcaw.*

THE BLOOD ON THEIR HANDS

BY ANNA-MARIE MCLEMORE

It begins with them looking inside me.

A scan of my body reveals a uterus so mutated it might qualify me for admission to Charles Xavier's School for Gifted Youngsters. The doctor draws a diagram of its topography on the back of a notepad left by a pharmaceutical rep. The cheerily printed logo in the upper corner is probably meant to suggest a life of playing with puppies and blowing out birthday candles. Instead, it just makes me think of the list of side effects announced, fast as an auctioneer's call, at the end of every commercial.

From that drawing—and this is the way I will remember it when I can't remember the name of my uterus's exact condition—it seems shaped like the locket my grandmother left me.

Poetic? It depends on what time of the month you ask me.

Dangerous? Not yet.

Detrimental when it comes to menstrual pain? Disastrously.

When the doctor says there is nothing truly wrong with me—not yet—her voice is so reassuring that I cannot bring myself to tell her that something *is* wrong. Two to three days a month are wrong. Two to three days when I feel like my uterus has been put in my mother's old-fashioned citrus press, which I now can't look at without thinking of my own body, my blood like the acid and pulp of a crushed lemon.

After more nights lost to screaming and the hottest baths I can stand, I work up the nerve to go back. This time, the doctor writes me an order for a prescription-strength dose of an over-the-counter painkiller, which I know will accomplish exactly nothing except letting me take one pill instead of three. But I do not mention that the equivalent dose barely touches that wringing pain. This is after working myself up in the waiting room, promising myself I will tell her I need *help*, that I cannot walk out of here with more recommendations for hot-water bottles and anti-inflammatories.

And yet I hear myself being silent.

I see my hand taking the prescription.

I feel myself nodding.

I am seldom more cowardly that I am in the face of doctors. It was true when I was fifteen, and mostly, it still is. I walk in ready to make demands, to *insist* the way I would for my husband or mother or best friend, and I walk out sure that I simply haven't been as open-minded about naproxen as I should be. After hearing the same recommendations from so many physicians, I tire and buckle and convince myself that if I work out more or wear red lipstick or listen to my mother more often that this thing I hate about myself will simply tire and buckle along with me.

The medication one doctor eventually puts me on, meant to regulate my cycles, gives me mood swings so fast and so severe that friends see my demeanor shift in the length of a single conversation, like the shadows of clouds moving overhead. In the span of a couple of minutes, I can go from burying my face in a neighbor's dinner-plate dahlias that bow over the sidewalk to sitting on the curb, clutching my ankles, because I am sure the grip of my hands is the only thing stopping my body from flying apart.

Against doctors' advice, I stop taking the medication.

It takes years of a plant-based diet and curanderismo-based remedios to repair the apparent damage done to my hair, skin, and brain chemistry.

When I am chosen for a random search of my suitcase, the TSA agent looks alarmed to see the impressive stock of pads and tampons taking up more space than my shoes (the statistically improbable frequency with which this random search happens likely has something to do with a profile I fit—Latina, small, young-looking, often clad in jeans and a sweatshirt, generally nervous around law enforcement). The four disposable heating pads I travel with at all times (the number I will need to cover the duration of my cramps) are more often than not flagged as suspicious on an X-ray, soliciting an explosives-residue test. When they're done, I thank the officers who have just shown the terminal my bras and toothbrush, and take with me what they must assume is some kind of pharmacy I've assembled in my carry-on.

A friend tries to teach me to use a menstrual cup, but a history of sexual assault makes me so tense about the prospect of shoving anything bigger than a super tampon into my vagina, I can't even relax enough to insert it.

When I shower, clots the size of walnuts and the color of plums fall out of me and break apart on the tile floor. When I'm not showering, I feel them dropping down and instantly soaking whatever tampon I've just put in.

When my body is being wrung out so hard that I'm sure something is ripping open, I genuinely consider what I might bang my head against hard enough to knock myself out. (Intense pain has a way of making such things seem like a logical idea.)

My abuela makes the sign of the cross on my forehead and tells me I will be healed. When the cramps come again to wring me out the next month, and the month after, and the month after, I do not tell her. My abuela's faith burns so hot, and I have seen so many of her prayers heal so many suffering bodies in her church, that I cannot help thinking the fault is purely mine.

I learn that society should raise men not to run at the thought of periods, that we must teach our brothers and sons and nephews to view our cycles as natural and even beautiful. But who knows when the hell that's going to happen, so instead I marry a trans guy who gets it because he's endured having one of his own. When we're moving into our first apartment, I make an offhand remark about my pad folding over while I'm wearing it, the adhesive sticking to half my pubic hair, how it feels like getting a bikini wax with masking tape.

He does not recoil. He does not exhibit the same horror my ex-boyfriends displayed at this part of me they considered crafted from blood and brujería. My husband just gives me a look of pained commiseration and says, "I *hate* that."

I accept the small mercies of friends who exist in that wringing-out space alongside me. They offer suggestions of spearmint tea and what to put in a bath. They offer them in a way that quietly makes clear that should my body not respond, there is no blame to assign. I look back at the nights I have curled up on the bathroom tile, blood on my hands because I cannot get up from the floor, cannot move the small distance to the cabinet that has the pads and tampons. And I realize that the doctors, as well as some of them may have meant, were taught medicine designed mostly with white, straight, cis, able bodies in mind, because our world has, for so long, been meant for white, straight, cis, able bodies. And I begin to believe that maybe, maybe, the fault is not with my body. Maybe it is not even with the blood-filled locket between my hips.

I live with a boy whose relationship with his own body is even more complicated than mine. He forgives me when he tries to bring me a cup of tea and I bite his hand, because something about the wrenching inside me makes me feral, and the fact that he knows this makes me too tired to hide it. He regards the sheer volume of blood my body crafts each month in a way that seems more awed than horrified, as though I have just pulled off a spell or a magic trick, and sometimes, sometimes, when the wringing has dulled enough to let me sleep, I believe him.

I learn to love certain things about my body—the beech-bark color of my hips, how my eyes are a dark enough brown to hide my pupils, the way my hair inexplicably gets more sun highlights on the bottom layer than the top. I learn to love these things even as I feel my body turning on me every three weeks,

> I ACCEPT THE SMALL MERCIES OF FRIENDS.

even as I hate the fact that my own biology can't even give me the courtesy of a twenty-eight-day-or-more cycle.

I adapt, as well as I can, to the fact that the particular hand biology dealt me will exact the price of between two and six days every calendar month, depending on how and where my cycle falls. Accounting for age and family history, chances are it will continue to do so for more than two decades to come. And because something inside me still bucks against that many days over that many years, I fight back, even if only in small stretches. I give speeches, win Irish dance medals, and smile at friends' weddings all while in the deepest moments of that pain, because there are some things worth pushing my body for, no matter what price it will demand for it in the days after. I accept the help of those around me who notice the signs of what happens to me because it happens to them too. (The first time I meet an author I've admired for years, she catches me wincing before a panel and quietly gives me an extra heating pad because I have burned through the entire set the TSA picked through days before.)

I learn, very slowly, to accept the help others offer.

I take small pieces of myself back.

I lose a little less of my life each month.

This is what I've learned from the weight of my own body dragging me to the floor two or three days out of every twenty-one:

You do the work of your own life, even if the truth of the world and your own body have worn you down so completely that you live some of that life on the floor.

If you cannot get up, you do the work anyway.

If you cannot get up, you work from the floor.

what are some normal side effects of menstruation?

Every person who menstruates experiences different side effects. Some may not experience anything at all, aside from discharge. Others may feel headaches, nausea, body pains (particularly breast tenderness or lower-back pain), cramps in the belly, and/or exhaustion. Some may experience appetite changes, desiring more or less food than normal. Sleep may change, as may skin, as it's more prone to acne. Many people may also become bloated.

There are many emotional side effects of menstruation as well: frustration, mood swings, sadness, low-grade depression, anxiety, and more.

It's possible for those who menstruate to *not* see menses every twenty-eight to thirty days. This can be normal and healthy, particularly for adolescents. It's common for runners, gymnasts, and other high-endurance athletes to experience athletic amenorrhea, which happens because of a shift in hormones in the body. If periods are irregular for more than three or four months, it's worth talking with a medical professional.

Another common phenomenon for those who menstruate is mittelschmerz, also known as ovulation pain or "middle pain." This sharp pain happens on one side of the abdomen, about two weeks before the start of one's period. It can be a jarring experience, but it's simply the body releasing an egg from an ovary. It can change from month to month in degrees of pain, and some people never feel it at all.

Although these are common menstrual experiences, any symptoms that disrupt one's daily activities are worth a trip to the doctor. A period can be annoying as much as it can be empowering and exciting, but it shouldn't derail your life completely.

BODY TALK

FAQS

FIVE THINGS PEOPLE WANT TO KNOW ABOUT THEIR JUNK (AND ARE AFRAID TO ASK)

BY I. W. GREGORIO

1. *I think my penis looks funny. Am I going to be OK?*

The short answer is this: almost certainly! If there's anything I've discovered after more than a decade of being a urologist, it's that there is a very wide definition of *normal* when it comes to human anatomy. Everyone's body looks different and behaves differently, and penises are no exception.

The most common and obvious way one penis can look different from another, of course, is whether it's circumcised or not. Basically, when a boy is born, he usually has a turtleneck-like cylinder of skin that covers the glans, or head, of the penis. For millennia, due to various cultural and religious reasons, some people have had their foreskin removed either in infancy or later in life. For an equally long time, circumcision has been controversial. The Greeks, for instance, considered it an aesthetic affront, preferring to "leave their genitals in their natural state," as per Herodotus. Nowadays, though about half the boys in America get circumcised just after birth, many parents choose not to circumcise, pointing out the risks of circumcision (including bleeding, possible loss of sexual sensation, and narrowing of the meatus—a.k.a. pee hole).

Some people can benefit from circumcision, however. In urology residency, we learn to perform circumcisions when boys and men need it for medical reasons, like prevention of UTIs, treatment of phimosis (inflammation of the foreskin that prevents a guy from pulling the foreskin back behind the glans), and removal of penile cancers, which are more common in uncircumcised men. There is data to suggest that circumcision can prevent STDs as well. Right now, no major medical society has come out clearly for or against circumcision, leaving the decision up to parents.

Other natural variations in penile anatomy exist, though they're rarely talked about. This can be a problem for the one in every three hundred boys who is born with hypospadias, a genital difference in which the urethral meatus isn't quite at the tip of the penis. Most of the time, the meatus is only a few millimeters away from where it's supposed to be, but sometimes it can be inches away—even underneath the scrotum. Often, hypospadias can come hand in hand with a condition called chordee, in which the penis can be twisted or curved. Usually this is painless, though the curvature may cause some discomfort during sex.

Neither chordee nor hypospadias are emergencies, with the main concerns being cosmetic appearance, the potential inability to pee straight, and in the case of really severe hypospadias, not being able to inseminate a partner through vaginal intercourse. Traditionally, pediatric urologists have offered parents early surgery on their children, due to concerns that any penile abnormality could cause emotional distress later on in life. A growing number of adults with hypospadias, however, argue that the risks of surgery are unacceptably severe for what is essentially a cosmetic procedure; this is supported by some medical research, which shows complication rates as high as 50 percent when the hypospadias is severe.

The bottom line is that variation in how things look down there is rarely life threatening. If something looks funny but doesn't hurt, things are probably going to be fine. Don't be afraid to seek out a urologist for reassurance if you're worried, though, and definitely see a doc if it hurts to pee or to get an erection.

2. *My balls hurt, but I'm too embarrassed to tell anyone about it. What should I do?*

IF SOMETHING LOOKS FUNNY BUT DOESN'T HURT, THINGS ARE PROBABLY GOING TO BE FINE.

Please, please, please do not be ashamed. There is one instance where it can be devastating if you try to tough it out and avoid medical attention, and that's something called testicular torsion, which is when the blood supply to the testicle gets cuts off when it twists around 720 degrees in your ball sack. It's basically like a heart attack in your scrotum, and that pain you feel is a disturbance in the force, as if millions of sperm are suddenly crying out in terror.

If you get yourself to an emergency room to see a urologist right away (and I'm talking minutes, not hours), they can sometimes do a surgery to untwist things and hopefully save the testicle. But you can't be afraid to say where the pain is. I've had one too many patients come into the emergency room complaining of belly pain, only to admit an hour or two into their stay that the pain was actually coming from their scrotum. Sometimes those two hours are just long enough that the testicle can't be saved—after four to six hours, the rate of salvage goes down, waaaay down.

3. *Is it OK for me to touch myself?*

Abso-freaking-lutely! In my work as a urologist, hardly a day goes by when I don't tell a young man to touch himself.

OK, so maybe my definition of *touching yourself* isn't exactly the one you're thinking about. What I encourage my young male patients to do is a testicular self-exam (TSE)—think of it as a guy's version of a breast exam. It's easy to do in the shower, and it's one instance in which self-screening is by far the most effective tool we have to catch cancer early, when it can be successfully treated.

Testicular cancer is one of the few tumors that's more common in young adults than it is in older people. It's also one of the most curable, so go to your doctor right away if you notice a change in how things feel down there. The key thing is that *you* know your body better than any physician or ultrasound. The typical testicle is soft and oval shaped, with a small ridge on the back that represents the epididymis, where the sperm is stored. Don't worry too much about lumps and bumps outside the testicle itself—99.9 percent of those are benign. Focus on the contours of the testicle; tumors are often irregular, more like the surface of a potato than that of a tomato. They're also usually quite firm, with a consistency that almost feels like that of a rubber bouncy ball.

4. *What's the best thing I can do for, uh, performance?*

This is going to sound super boring, but clean living is honestly the best prescription for any guy who's looking to get it on.

These are the biggest causes of erectile dysfunction in youngish men:

- Smoking. Basically, cigarettes are the anti-Viagra. They screw up the blood vessels that lead to erection.

- Alcohol. The conventional wisdom is that alcohol, a depressant, can impact the brain signals that regulate sexual arousal, and it also shunts blood away from your nether regions. While some data shows that moderate drinking might not affect erectile function, sexual dysfunction is higher in men who abuse alcohol.

- Unhealthy diets and inactivity. Overeating and lack of exercise contribute to obesity (which can affect testosterone levels) and diabetes (which can affect both the blood vessels and the nerves that contribute to sexual function).

- Recreational drugs. Some studies have shown that marijuana, especially, can make it more difficult for men to get hard-ons, but the evidence isn't 100 percent conclusive.

One of the most important—and overlooked—factors for young people when it comes to sexual function is mental health. People who are depressed can have a lower sex drive and are more likely to be on medications that can impair arousal, ejaculation, and orgasm.

The take-home message is that the best way to ensure good performance is to exercise, eat and drink well, and take care of both your body *and* your mind.

5. *If size doesn't really matter, then what does?*

I'm so glad you asked! If you come out of reading this essay remembering one thing, I hope it's this: you don't need a penis to pleasure your partner.

In my practice, I see thousands of men a year. Some of them are eighty years old with heart problems and can barely walk. Some of them have had prostate surgery that damaged the nerves that lead to erection. Some of them have had penile cancer and needed to have their penises amputated. Some of them are veterans whose genitalia or spinal cords were damaged by IEDs. Some of them are transgender men who weren't born with male anatomy.

All these people, though, have the potential to have meaningful sex lives. Though no one is denying that penises can be quite useful, they aren't necessary to give others orgasms. There are lots of ways to get someone off, including oral or digital stimulation.

Every person on this earth experiences pleasure in subtly different ways. The keys to making sure that everyone has a good time are honesty, an open mind, and communication.

That's all for now, folks. Be healthy, be happy, and don't be afraid to reach out to your friendly neighborhood urologist if you have any more questions!

CRY LIKE A GIRL

BY KATE HART

"If it *really* hurt, you'd come up off the table when I pressed here."

It did hurt. I'd just confirmed that by saying, "Yeah, it hurts." Had I realized getting further care depended on my level of histrionics, I might have put on a better show.

But that's not really my style, and besides, I was too tired to shriek and writhe in pain. It had been a week since my surgery—my sixth overall and my third to remove endometriosis.[1] Recovery was not going well, and even if I'd had the energy to launch a full-scale pain production, I couldn't breathe well enough to scream anyway.

This doctor was in the room only because I'd already done something out of character: I'd cried when the resident said she couldn't help me. They were tears of frustration and rage, not pain, but they'd convinced her to bring in the head of the department. Both of them were filling in for the two *other* doctors who'd actually performed my surgery the previous Monday. I'd come to their clinic, with its more specialized expertise, in a bigger city, hoping for answers that multiple gynecologists at home couldn't provide.

Instead, my stomach had swollen to the size of two watermelons after the surgery, so enormous that on Tuesday morning, my hometown emergency room had rushed me to a bed, thinking I was pregnant. I was diagnosed

---

1 "Endometriosis is a condition where tissue similar to the lining of the uterus (the endometrial stroma and glands, which should only be located inside the uterus) is found elsewhere in the body." The lesions "can be found anywhere in the pelvic cavity," as well as in "caesarian-section scars, laparoscopy/laparotomy scars, on the bladder, on the bowel, on the intestines, colon, appendix, and rectum. . . . In even more rare cases, endometriosis has been found inside the vagina, inside the bladder, on the skin, in the lung, spine, and brain." Unfortunately, "many myths and misconceptions about endometriosis still persist, even in the medical literature." (Source: http://endometriosis.org/endometriosis)

with kidney failure, treated for two days, released, then readmitted on Saturday when it started all over again. The ER told me that no doctor was going to want to take responsibility for another surgeon's patient—their goal was just to stabilize me so that I could make the ninety-minute drive back to the city.

And now, after an exhausting week on and off a catheter, a decade of chronic pain, and a lifetime of trying to be tough, I wasn't wailing or moaning. I was telling them very plainly that I'd been through multiple surgeries before, and this level of recovery pain wasn't normal, nor was the inability to pee on my own.

But they couldn't hear what I was saying. "We can't give you more painkillers," the doctor said. "Opiates are constipating." The fact that I hate pain pills and didn't want them in the first place didn't seem to matter. They were convinced my problem was a run-of-the-mill digestive issue, anyway. "Your best bet is to go back to the hotel and take more laxatives."

"She tried that last night, but it didn't work," my husband said. A sad truth of my experience being a female patient is that bringing a man with me is often helpful, and after months of attending appointments, he knew the drill.[2] "She spent the night in the fetal position on the bathroom floor."

"Well," the doctor said, "I'm not sure what else to tell you."

"At what point do we take her to the emergency room?" my husband demanded. "Because that's where we were headed when you opened up this appointment."

"When the pain becomes unmanageable," the doctor said.

"That's why we're here," I said through gritted teeth.

"Oh." The doctor glanced at the resident. "Well, I guess I could admit you to the hospital," he said, as if that would convince me laxatives really were the way to go.

---

2 While I recognize and respect a full spectrum of gender identities, medical professionals I've seen have always assumed a simplistic binary approach, which is reflected here.

An hour later, I had a bed and an IV drip with a non-opiate painkiller. Blood tests revealed my kidneys were failing yet again—and as a side effect, I'd developed an obstructed bowel that no amount of Miralax was going to cure. It was several more days before a urologist finally ran the right imaging test and discovered the surgeon had burned a hole in my bladder.

On Saturday, I had surgery number seven.

"It's nothing personal. We just wanted to take a smaller trip without all the whining."

My senior year of high school, my friends and I skipped the stereotypical Panama City Beach spring break and drove to the Havasupai reservation in Arizona, where we backpacked to Havasu Falls. I'd grown up camping and fishing, but I'd never backpacked before, much less hiked twenty miles. There were ten of us—three girls, seven boys—and only two of us had technical wilderness training, but we survived the trip. I lived on trail rations, carried a pack, slept on the ground, shit in the woods, and alongside my best girlfriend, conquered the almost-vertical last mile back to the canyon rim. As far as I knew, everyone had a pretty good time, and I was proud of myself for making it through.

Until a few of the guys planned another trip that summer. And I was not invited.

Because of the whining.

Only one girl was deemed "tough enough" to accompany them, a friend who hadn't gone on spring break. She was tougher than I was, no doubt—so tough that when her new boots caused extreme blisters, she kept hiking without complaint until her shoes filled with blood. When they got home, the boys waxed rhapsodic about what a badass she was . . . and, behind her back, said it was a good thing she didn't get an infection or gangrene.

The following summer, they took a boys' trip to Wyoming. No girls allowed.

Let me be clear: these guys are still some of my closest friends. As teens, we were all swimming in the same toxic sea of patriarchy and sexism; as adults, we've found our ways to the other shore. We're godparents to each other's children, attendants in each other's weddings, and executors of each other's wills. I even married one of them, despite the fact that he tagged along on the all-boys trip, where they were almost eaten to death by mosquitoes. Which I still think they fully deserved.

"If this was a spinal headache," the doctor told me after I gave birth, "you'd be sobbing in pain."

My hospital room was completely dark because opening my eyes was torture. "This doesn't feel like my usual migraines," I said. I couldn't even bend my neck to look down at my second child as I held him.

"Well, spinal headaches can be a side effect of having an epidural," he said, "but that can't be it. You'd be throwing up if it was."

I wasn't sobbing, and I wasn't throwing up. I neither cry nor barf easily. But I *was* in the ER the next day, nursing my newborn while we tried to convince yet more doctors that I needed treatment.

You may be noticing a pattern here.

My husband and I were the first of our high school crew to have children. We had get-togethers when people came home for the holidays, and while whipping out a boob to feed my kid in front of everyone made me hyperconscious that I was decidedly not "one of the boys" anymore, something about having let half the hospital look at my nether regions during the course of pregnancy had made me a little less self-conscious overall.

Besides, having had an emergency C-section meant I got to tell everyone about how the doctors piled all my internal organs on my chest during the surgery.

Sure, I was just lying there, but it still seemed pretty badass.

It was easier for them to understand than the challenge we'd faced to get pregnant in the first place. After years of taking precautions against the terror of getting knocked up, it was a shock to realize my body actually sucked at the task. Clinical depression had already forced me to reckon with the fact that no amount of effort or focus could force one's brain chemicals to behave, but applying that lesson to the rest of my body was difficult. No amount of toughness will bully your ovaries into producing decent eggs. And when infertility treatments finally work and it comes time to give birth, you can't force the baby to turn itself head down—particularly when no one notices he's breech until you're already dilated to ten centimeters.

"I could smell the burning flesh when they cauterized the incision," I said, and that seemed to be a crowd-pleaser.

A year after my second child was born, I noticed a lump on my C-section scar. It was small, under the skin, and a little painful, making it difficult to wear anything tight on my waist.

"It's probably a hernia," my OB-GYN said, and she sent me to a surgeon.

"It's definitely a hernia," the surgeon said, and he cut me open.

It was not a hernia.

It was endometrial tissue that was growing in the scar, assumed to have escaped during the earlier procedures. "It's not likely to come back," he assured me.

It came back.

Fast-forward through several years, in which I struggled with unexplained spotting, ridiculously long periods, hot flashes, crazy mood swings, and stomach upset of various kinds. I had chronic urinary tract infections and back pain. I had an ovarian cyst or two, but they never burst, so no one seemed too worried. I took a variety of birth control pills and every dosage of antidepressant possible. I was tired, and my body hurt unpredictably—then, worse, constantly. I could barely get off the couch most days, much less parent those kids I wanted so badly.

Sometimes I sought treatment, and sometimes I just tried to tough it out. When the doctors seem stymied, there's not much else to do. Finally, once again, I ended up in the ER. Because I didn't seem to be in extreme pain, it took them eight hours to see me and diagnose bladder spasms.

A urology follow-up showed nothing.

Meanwhile, a new lump was growing on the other end of my C-section scar, and this time my gynecologist said it was unrelated to my other issues and not worth investigating.

When I finally insisted that maybe, just maybe, this was more endometrial tissue, and pointed out that my ovarian cysts had been endometriomas, her response was almost angry. "We can do laparoscopic surgery, but I can't remove the lump that way. And if it doesn't work, we'll probably have to do [a drug I'm not naming, because I don't like lawsuits], which puts you into premature menopause."

"That drug has horrible side effects," I said, "and I'm a little young to go through menopause."

"Your other option is a hysterectomy."

I already knew that despite popular belief, a hysterectomy doesn't cure or even treat endometriosis. So I got a new doctor.

But my new doctor screwed stuff up too, so I got another.

And another. And another.

My oldest child was only four when my endometriosis symptoms started to show up in earnest. By the time he and his brother were old enough to retain real memories, I was already sidelined with chronic pain. When I was able to join them on hikes, it was a notable event, but always a short one. At some point

I realized that my children had no idea I used to be tough. They'd never seen me as anything but Mommy, that woman that Daddy fetches things and cooks for.

And after the botched surgery and bladder repair, things only got worse. Pelvic pain and muscle spasms were frequent, and I spent anywhere from thirty minutes to two hours in the bathroom daily. Travel, hiking, gardening—everything I enjoyed was difficult at best. On top of it all, there was an unrelenting mental fog that made reading and writing almost impossible. In the greatest of ironies, I had to give up hosting an interview series called Badass Ladies You Should Know.

Friends and family tried to spin the situation, assuring me that just having survived the experience meant I was super tough. "OK, but did you *die*?" became our household catchphrase, putting any petty annoyances into perspective. But lying on the couch for months did not feel hard-core. Buying a used RV so I'd have easy access to a bathroom while camping was not exactly badass. And yes, discussing my bowel movements with perfect strangers, much less undergoing imaging tests for them, was pretty tough, but not in the way I'd always aspired to. The ultimate insult added to injury was that all these issues were thanks to my "lady parts."

I think childbearing is one of the most badass things a person can do, and even if I'd known this would be the result, I still would've gone through it to have my kids. But I didn't know, and it's not because I didn't research or ask for help. I didn't know endometriosis existed or that it might be related to C-sections. I didn't know that the walls between various pelvic organs can weaken, letting them collapse into one another, and I didn't know that fibroids and adenomyosis and Crohn's disease and any number of other conditions can all overlap.

I didn't know that gynecologists get, on average, at least a year less surgical training than other specialists, and I didn't know so many of them are woefully behind on the research for treating those diseases.

I didn't know how much doctors don't know. And I didn't know that the ultimate test of my toughness would be advocating for myself.

I had to be the whiner. I had to make myself heard.

"I don't want you to become a professional patient."

My eighth surgery revealed issues the other doctors had missed: more spots of endometriosis, a pelvic prolapse that hadn't been addressed, and surprise, the need for a hysterectomy, though not for the reason originally thought—it turned out that in addition to being halfway overrun with scar tissue, my uterus was also glued to my bladder.

Finding this specialist had been a challenge. I'd joined a research group on Facebook, of all places, and learned an enormous amount about my condition, the issues that often accompany it, and the failure of the medical community to adjust treatment protocols.[3] The group kept a list of specialists who had proven results, and the closest one to me was six hours away, in Dallas. He took my insurance, but then my insurance changed, and I had to find a new plan, which took months.

But besides validating my symptoms and my pain, my new specialist also said one of the most helpful things I've ever heard from a medical professional. While he agreed with others in my life who thought I should be putting together a lawsuit, he understood why I was reluctant. "You definitely have

_____

3 Nancy's Nook Endometriosis Education is a private Facebook group that can be joined by anyone, but be sure to answer the preliminary questions, which help keep out scammers. This is not a support group, so don't expect hand-holding—it's a self-education resource with a library of files to help you make informed decisions about your care.

some trauma from all of this," he said. "And it's OK to just take care of yourself. You can't let your life revolve around being sick."

Not every chronic-illness patient has the luxury of decentering their illness, and I'm all too aware that even with expert treatment, endometriosis can come back. I'll always have pain issues regardless, even with pelvic physical therapy, which has helped tremendously.

But I'm taking his advice so far as I can. I'm glad to have some advice worth following.

In retrospect, maybe I should have cried like a girl.

It's easy now to see all the places I screwed up. I should have known then what I know from research now. I should have left this doctor earlier and demanded this consult or that. I should have put my pride aside and demonstrated pain in a way doctors expected.

Hindsight is twenty-twenty and whatnot. But it's hard to see the forest for the trees when you're being forced to find your own way.

On the anniversary of my botched surgery, I celebrated my survival by hiking at Palo Duro with my best friend from high school, the woman who had climbed that final spring break stretch out of Havasu Falls by my side. It was a tough hike, and near the end, my husband took my picture as I flexed a not-so-muscular biceps, while my kids marveled, since they'd never seen me hike six miles before.

It was also a tough drive home. My weak pelvic muscles made their objections to the challenge well known, wrapping my entire middle in ache while demanding I stop to pee every thirty minutes.

I didn't cry or vomit. I did admit I needed a heating pad and some low-octane painkillers. And when we got home, I let myself rest for a few days.

I was proud of myself for making it that far.

what is a pink tax?

Have you ever been to the store to pick up something like deodorant and noticed that the prices for "women's" deodorant and "men's" deodorant differ? This is the pink tax, and it's a form of sexism (and even classism!) that charges those who identify as women—and purchase products marketed to women—more money for the same, or sometimes even a lesser, product as those marketed to men.

In 2015, the New York City Department of Consumer Affairs found that 42 percent of the products they looked at included higher prices for the "women's" version than the "men's" and that this starts young. Baby products and items for young girls are priced higher than those for boys, and on average, when a woman purchases products like shampoo, razors, body wash, etc., she pays 13 percent more. Most of the time, the only difference between products is the color or shape of the bottle or packaging.

A few cents' difference might not seem like much, but not only does it add up, it can also impact self-esteem, particularly for those in lower socioeconomic classes. For those already struggling to make ends meet, spending extra cents to buy essentials might mean going without or feeling forced to skip what might be a small indulgence in a particular item that makes them feel good in their bodies.

Many states in the US are fighting back against the pink tax, but you may still encounter it at the store where you purchase your essentials. If so, you can simply choose not to purchase the items with the higher price, as the components of the less-pricey "men's" products are nearly—if not entirely—identical to the ones in the pink or sparkly packages.

BODY TALK

FAQS

SISTERHOOD, BLOOD, AND BOOBS AT THE LONDON MARATHON 2015

BY KIRAN/MADAME GANDHI

The marathon was everything. I trained for a year and then it happened. And truly it was one of the most profound experiences of my life. I ran with two of the most important women in my life, Ana and Meredith, and we didn't leave each other's side once, from start to finish. We crossed the finish line hand in hand. We raised $6,000 collectively for Breast Cancer Care. And we ran the whole way without stopping. London is one of the world's best marathons because so many people come out for it—the sidelines are packed for the entire 26.2 miles and Londoners' signs are hilarious. There are crazy people running without shoes or wearing tutus or carrying forty pounds on their back, and there are dance parties along the way. If I had to summarize my experience, though, the marathon was about family and feminism.

It was about family because my dad and brother came out and it was the best. My dad made T-shirts, and they both wore them and met me at the breast cancer cheer points at miles 9 and 18.5! Ana's mom and sister were there, too, and supported us with the best screams and hugs throughout the race! I remember segmenting parts of the marathon in my head: get to mile 6, then to mile 9 to see family, then to the halfway point at mile 13.1, then to mile 18.5 to see my family again, and then to the finish line at 26.2. At the end of the marathon we were greeted by so many of our London-based friends at the Breast Cancer Care after-party at the Sofitel hotel—it was so well-organized and fun and family-oriented and just so magical and special. I walked away from this experience understanding how much being there for someone else in a totally selfless way can carry them through a difficult time. I felt my friends' support, and that bond is now for life.

It was about feminism because I RAN THE WHOLE MARATHON WITH MY PERIOD BLOOD RUNNING DOWN MY LEGS. I got my flow the morning of, and it was a total disaster but I didn't want to clean it up. It would have been way too uncomfortable to worry about a tampon for 26.2 miles. I thought, *If there's one person society won't fuck with, it's a marathon runner. If there's one way to transcend oppression, it's to run a marathon in whatever way you want.* On the marathon course, sexism can be overcome. It's where the stigma of a womxn's period is irrelevant, and we can rewrite the rules as we choose. It's where a woman's comfort supersedes that of the observer. I ran with blood dripping down my legs for sisters who don't have access to tampons and sisters who, despite cramping and pain, hide it away and pretend like it doesn't exist. I ran to say it does exist, and we overcome it every day. The marathon was radical and absurd and bloody in ways I couldn't have imagined before the day of the race.

From a young age, women are told that their main value to society is to look beautiful, consumable, f*ckable. A period doesn't fit into this image, so it is made taboo. So much so that parents have an awkward time discussing it with children, period commercials are all about concealing yourself or saving yourself from "embarrassment" (they don't even show blood in a commercial about blood—they show a metaphorical blue liquid!), and girls are quiet about periods when boys are nearby, even though it shouldn't be something to be ashamed of.

While I am not advocating for free-bleeding, I am advocating for it to be OK for women and trans folks to speak comfortably and honestly about their own bodies, to ask for medicine and not have to pretend they have a stomachache when they are experiencing menstrual cramps. To not fear someone will make fun of them for PMSing instead of asking how to help, and to ask for a

> I AM ADVOCATING FOR IT TO BE OK FOR WOMEN AND TRANS FOLKS TO SPEAK COMFORTABLY AND HONESTLY ABOUT THEIR OWN BODIES.

short break in school or at the office if that's what they need to deliver their best work. Steve Jobs and Mark Zuckerberg have both said the reason they wear almost identical outfits every day is to have one less decision to make, freeing up the mental capacity to handle one more decision relating to their work. Just think, every day women have to worry about hair, makeup, weight, clothing, shoes, periods, and general desirability, instead of being given the freedom to just get on with their work. When we aren't beautiful, we aren't as desirable even when we are awesome at what we do, and when we are super beautiful, we aren't taken seriously.

Women, biologically, are given traits that are attractive. We don't need any more. We have things like eyelashes, hair, and breasts, which are already feminine traits that make us naturally attractive. We should be able to love these things about ourselves, eat healthily, and focus on our passions and work. Periods are an important part of this conversation because the reason there's stigma around them is that they're not sexy and therefore not acceptable to talk about. For this reason, my marathon run was about reclaiming the fact that it is not my job to look sexy for others' public consumption. My job on the marathon course was to choose what was right for me in that moment and to complete the 26.2-mile race in the safest and healthiest way possible.

In the developing world, period stigma is even worse. I don't know why we don't talk more about the link between women's economic oppression and period stigma. This is the pattern I see: Girls are not allowed to talk about or reveal that they experience a monthly biological process called menstruation. We then make it extremely expensive, unsustainable, and inaccessible to actually conceal it. Pads are a luxury for most rural communities, and tampons are not a practical solution for most societies that are extremely protective of women's virginity—this kind of penetration would not be encouraged or allowed. Because periods are difficult to talk about and expensive to clean up, most girls in these communities end up staying at home monthly, missing school and growing up feeling shame, instead of confidence, about their bodies. And missing school means they don't graduate with the same education that the boys have, immediately putting them at an economic disadvantage but also an emotional one—if you feel like you don't have any power, you will act like you don't have any power. This can happen to anyone—regardless of gender. It perpetuates a cycle of women having low self-esteem, a lack of information, and a lack of physical and emotional resources to lift themselves out of poverty.

Although menstruation stigma is only one of many systemic factors that perpetuate gender inequality, I find it to be a rather large one that we frequently ignore. My run was ultimately about using shock factor to create dialogue around menstrual health as well as providing comfort so that women can start to own the narrative of their own bodies. Speaking about an issue is the only way to combat its silence, and dialogue is the only way for innovative solutions to occur.

I could never have expected the international viral reaction that resulted online several months after my race. This reaction taught us two things: that period stigma runs deep and that we have a lot of work to do as a society to build a world that is more loving and inclusive of women's bodies.

A version of this essay was previously published on MadameGandhi.blog.

THINGS YOU CANNOT SEE

SOME THINGS ABOUT THE EXPERIENCE OF HAVING A HUMAN BODY AREN'T VISIBLE,

like our brain function or our inner thoughts. In this section, we'll explore the challenges of existing in a body when something is different but it's a difference we can't necessarily see.

Different, of course, means that it deviates from the western ideal of how a body should function. The word *different* is too often used by people who misunderstand the variety of ways in which a body operates.

This section explores not only the experiences of having an invisible or chronic illness but also what it means when your sexual experiences lie outside what's often seen as the singular norm. It also delves into how altering our appearance isn't about how we want to present ourselves to the world, but rather about how we hope to make our bodies a little more magical for ourselves.

WHEN YOU'RE "BROKEN" LIKE ME

BY amanda lovelace

It was mere days after I got engaged to my now spouse.

At the risk of sounding cliché, the proposal felt like something out of a storybook.

While we were visiting family in Michigan, my partner, Cyrus, walked me down to what I always called "our fairy-tale bridge," which overlooked the water and the local ferry system. After a few minutes reminiscing about our years-long friendship and partnership, they reached into their bag and pulled out one of our mutually favorite books, *Clockwork Princess* by Cassandra Clare, and got down on one knee.

When they opened up the front cover, they revealed a space perfectly carved out for a ring.

With the sunlight reflecting off it, I realized it was the amethyst clad-dagh ring I had designed—the same one I had always dreamed would be on my finger.

Now it was.

It was supposed to be the happiest time in my life.

Until I checked my messages on Tumblr, where I ran a book blog:

"You're engaged? I thought you were asexual?"

"How can you be engaged if you're ace?"

"You don't deserve them."

"They're going to leave you if you don't drop this 'demisexual' nonsense."

Many of the messages were sent from anonymous accounts, but some weren't. Some of them were sent from people I interacted with on a regular basis. Those people were so unashamed of their thoughts, they kept their comments attached to their names and faces.

My heart raced.

I imagined my stomach like a dryer: rolling, rolling, rolling.

One of my greatest fears was coming true: part of the queer community I thought I had found safe haven in was turning against me.

All the acceptance and positivity the community had taught me was dissolving before my eyes. It was something I couldn't wrap my head around. I simply couldn't cope with it.

Maybe, just maybe, the commenters—and their comments—were right.

I was broken after all.

Growing up, I knew a few things about myself to be true: I loved Harry Potter more than anything else, I was going to be a writer, and I didn't often feel sexually attracted to others.

Back then, I didn't have the language to describe the last certainty, but I was, without a doubt, on the asexual spectrum.

And because I didn't have that language, I spent so much of my life pretending.

I pretended to agree with my peers about which celebrities they found *hot* or *sexy*. Looking back now, I realize I found some of these celebrities to be aesthetically pleasing, but sexual feelings had absolutely nothing to do with it.

I pretended to have more crushes than I did. On the rare occasion I did begin to have genuine feelings for someone, sexual attraction followed only after knowing them on a much deeper level, and usually for an extended period of time. I thought this was how it worked for everyone—turns out I was wrong! Though I didn't know it yet, this made me demisexual.

I pretended to be curious about my body in the same way everyone else seemed to be curious about theirs.

I pretended to exclusively like boys even after I realized that gender had no bearing on whether I could find someone attractive. I didn't have the knowledge to understand that, on top of being asexual, I was also pansexual, let alone the knowledge that you can be on the spectrum of two sexualities at the same time.

To top it all off, I never saw these pieces of myself reflected in any of my favorite fictional characters, at least not until my late teens.

It became even more complicated when I began dating. I didn't have a full grasp on my own sexual feelings, so how was I going to find the words to explain them to someone else? And in such a hypersexualized society, would my partner believe that not only was sexual attraction a rare occurrence in my life, but even when I did feel attraction toward someone else, the desire to have sex with them wasn't there most of the time?

The answer was no.

Most of the time, they did not understand.

Just as I had anticipated, it was difficult for anyone to wrap their head around the idea that I could love them dearly yet not give them what they saw as the ultimate portrayal of love: sex. This led to many an awkward conversation, and it also led to arguments about their need to feel desired. One partner told me I just had to keep masturbating until my body magically "turned on" like a computer, never to power off again. Unfortunately, this lack of understanding also led to a number of traumatic experiences that I didn't even realize were assault until later on.

Since I was a little girl, I'd wanted that great fairy-tale love for my life, but I started to believe that maybe being alone would be safer for me.

One day, I was feeling brave enough, so I confided in my best friend.

I told her I mostly had no interest in sex.

I told her I had no interest in exploring my body.

I told her I understood that other people wanted those things but that I'd rather be doing something—no, *anything* else.

There, it was done.

Mountains were lifted from my shoulders.

I no longer had to hide who I was, at least not from those I loved and trusted the most. If anyone was going to accept me as I was, it was going to be her, wasn't it?

"I feel so incredibly sorry for you," she told me.

I didn't respond.

I let other people convince me that I wasn't normal.

That I was a broken thing that couldn't be fixed.

I kept on living my life, pretending I wasn't queer, and it was the hardest thing I've ever had to do. But I was terrified of the way the world would react to my identity. The violence, the ignorance—it didn't seem worth it anymore, so I disconnected myself from it.

If no one knew it was part of me, then it could no longer hurt me.

It was while I was running my aforementioned book blog on Tumblr that I started to see posts about asexuality floating around.

It surprised me how many other people were relating to them just as much as I was. But I didn't feel like I personally connected to the term *asexual* until I learned that it wasn't just one thing, but an entire spectrum with many points on it, including something called *demisexual*, otherwise known as someone who usually doesn't experience sexual attraction to another person until after they've formed a strong emotional bond.

That . . . was me.

It was exactly me.

When I came out as *demisexual* on my blog, and then later as *demi-pansexual* (a common term used to indicate someone who identifies as both

> I'D DISCOVERED A PART OF MYSELF I'D BEEN SEARCHING FOR MY ENTIRE LIFE.

demisexual as well as *pansexual*), I could practically hear the cheers of the community from different cities, states, countries, continents. There were some innocent questions from others, but mostly just joy that I'd discovered a part of myself I'd been searching for my entire life.

My book blog was about how much words had changed and shaped my life, and that's exactly what happened then, too.

It was with the same blogging community I fangirled about *The Hunger Games* with.

Katniss was someone I could relate to on so many levels: I was antisocial; I didn't feel fit to be in the spotlight, let alone to be the one who saves the day; and I would fight fiercely on behalf of my loved ones. Though it was never confirmed in the text of the story, I always felt like there was another thing we had in common: we were both on the asexual spectrum.

It turned out that other people in the community felt the exact same way I did, and it was through Katniss, our unconventional hero, that we saw ourselves and found validation.

If she could fight for justice and win, then couldn't we do the same?

Somewhere down the line, one of my oldest friends became my partner, and unlike the ones who came before them, they took the time and care to understand the intricacies of my sexuality, even as I was still navigating it myself. I referred to them as my Peeta, and they referred to me as their Katniss.

I felt safe enough with them to say yes when they took me down to that fairy-tale bridge and presented me with that ring, and none of the events that unfurled afterward can ever take that moment away from me.

Acephobia is an ugly, insidious monster.

Sometimes people who don't understand asexuality decide to other us, to dehumanize us. Some decide we're experiencing an illness of some sort, not an identity.

Other times, people who *do* understand asexuality decide we aren't queer, because we haven't suffered enough to their liking. Despite what some may think, many of us do suffer, but I don't think that should define our right to identify as queer.

When my community turned on me that day, it took everything in me to not turn my back on myself again.

As my tears dried, I told myself I hadn't come so far in my own journey of acceptance just to tiptoe back into the closet and turn off the light. The people who hurled their hatred at me didn't represent the whole community—only a small (but loud) part of it. Despite what they had done, I still had a support system within the community that never faltered and a partner who offered words of affirmation whenever I was in doubt. No one ever gets to take away the love I feel for myself and the pride I feel for my identity—not even if they were part of the community that helped me get here in the first place.

At the beginning of *Harry Potter and the Sorcerer's Stone*, Harry lives in a cramped, uncomfortable closet in a home filled with quite a few abusers, but at the end of *Harry Potter and the Deathly Hallows*, Harry is living a joyous life and no longer has to be afraid. Along the way, he creates a found family out of his friends, and it's with them that he creates a life in which he no longer has to hide from his villains.

It took a long time to find my people, but I did.

We eat together. We laugh together. We create together. We have our disagreements. But they never question my sexuality (surprise: some of us share the same ones!) or my life choices. Best of all, they've never once made me feel like I don't belong or like I'm broken, like I used to feel all those years ago.

I still got the great fairy tale I'd always wanted, and I do it on my terms now.

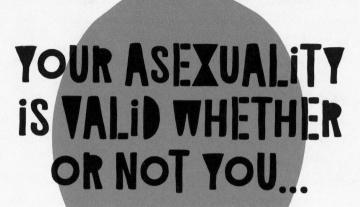

YOUR ASEXUALiTY iS VALiD WHETHER OR NOT YOU...

by amanda loveface

GO ON DATES.

HAVE SEX.

HAVE A SEX DRIVE.

MASTURBATE.

HAVE A SEXUAL OR
ROMANTIC PARTNER.

ENJOY ROMANCE NOVELS.

HAVE EXPERIENCED
SEXUAL ATTRACTION.

WANT TO GET MARRIED.

HAVE AN OTP.

WANT TO HAVE KIDS.

HAVE EXPERIENCED TRAUMA.

FEEL VALID.

BENEATH THE SURFACE

BY ABBY SAMS

"But you don't *look* sick."

The words hit me for the hundredth time, intended to be a compliment but never taken as such. Instead, they remind me of the blatant issue society has toward people with invisible illnesses and the deep-rooted ignorance on the subject of disability as a whole.

An invisible illness is one in which the patient's appearance does not signal to a bystander that they are disabled or ill. This lack of visual representation too often leads able-bodied people to make snap judgments that may be incorrect or downright rude. Since more than 10 percent of the United States population has an invisible illness, why do we still have to fight through a world that is often uneducated and impolite toward the chronically ill community?

I have Ehlers-Danlos syndrome as well as reflex sympathetic dystrophy. Both conditions are incurable and cause me to be in a great amount of constant pain in my legs as well as the rest of my body. I wear knee braces and ankle-foot orthotics to help reduce the pain and the risk of dislocation when I walk. More often than not, I opt for my wheelchair when I go out for long periods of time.

On the days I wear all my braces, I am constantly met with "What happened?!" by strangers. There is this idea that if you don't actually look sick—because you're young, pretty, fit, etc.—then you must be able to get better. The assumption that whatever is "wrong" with me isn't permanent is the biggest problem with the "you don't look sick" mentality. Because I look like a generally healthy young adult, even in my wheelchair, it leads people to believe that my condition must be curable or, better yet, that they have the solution.

My inbox is flooded with links to diet plans, yoga classes, and essential oils that are supposed to cure me. I'm constantly told I'm "too pretty to be in a wheelchair" or "too young to be disabled" when the truth is that I can be pretty *and* be in a wheelchair and I can be young *and* disabled. Disability does not discriminate; people do.

When people say, "But you don't look sick," they are suggesting that being sick or disabled or chronically ill is a bad thing or that it makes you less of a person. It's supposed to make the receiver feel better about themselves. As children, many of us were raised to not stare, not point, not acknowledge people with illnesses or disabilities because it was "rude." Unfortunately, those behaviors taught us that people with illnesses and disabilities were meant to be overlooked and avoided and weren't meant to be talked to. The general lack of education about disability only furthers the stigma.

"But you don't look sick" can also be an accusatory statement. People with invisible disabilities and illnesses are accused of "faking" and "lying" about them.

When I received my first (of many) windshield notes accusing me of faking my disability, I did not leave my house for weeks afterward, because I was too afraid to face the public. What if it was more than a note next time? What if I was alone? Because there is so little education on what disability and chronic illness actually look like, many people believe any deviation from a stereotype *must* be fake.

These stereotypes grow because of the severe lack of representation—especially accurate representation—of disabilities across the spectrum in TV shows, in movies, and on the runway.

Wheelchair users are often shown as completely paralyzed. Deaf characters usually either are profoundly deaf or are completely "cured" when they use a hearing aid. Diabetes patients (both type 1 and type 2) are either severely overweight or extremely malnourished. The representations of invisible illnesses fed to the public are starkly one sided, and whether or not those establishments know it or care, they perpetuate the idea that those depictions are the only true versions.

The truth is, nearly 90 percent of wheelchair users have at least some function in their legs. But when the only representation of wheelchair users in media is complete paralysis, able-bodied people will virtually always ask a wheelchair user if they are "better" or "cured" or "faking" because they moved their leg or walked out of their car to grab their wheelchair. Ambulatory wheelchair users will hear shouts of "It's a miracle" when they brave the public. And smartphones with the ability to record at a moment's notice allow "miracle" videos to spread like wildfire on social media.

For the invisibly ill, harassment is a regular occurrence, and fear becomes instilled in our hearts. There have been many times when I've visited a store alone and, once there, decided to use my wheelchair so that I could explore it more easily. But because I've had to walk around my car to get my wheelchair from the trunk, I've been confronted by strangers in the store who saw me walking in the parking lot. They come up to me, furious that I would "fake such a serious disability just because I'm too lazy to walk." Or they tell me that I should "leave that spot for someone who's actually disabled" before stomping away in a rage without giving me the opportunity to explain or educate. These experiences have forced me to learn how to put my wheelchair together from the driver's seat, or to go shopping with friends so they can get my chair for me—all so I can avoid the conflict and the hate that too often come with trying to exist in an uneducated world.

Many disabled people hoped the book *Me Before You*, and later the movie adaptation of it, would be the representation we had been waiting for. However, that was not the case. In the story, the disabled protagonist's caretaker falls in love with him. He doesn't believe they can live a fulfilling and good life together because of his disability, so he kills himself to "free" her from living a compromised life. This harmful narrative perpetuates and feeds the notion that disabled people cannot have full lives. I'm a young disabled woman who is engaged, and this kind of narrative has been used against my own extremely loving relationship. Many people have told me that my fiancé should leave me because I'm disabled and he shouldn't have to "deal with that." We both want to, and can, live fulfilling lives with love and happiness and adventure with one another. I do not experience life less simply because I am disabled.

The "but you don't look sick" mentality is one that can and will be changed. First, though, we need to break the stigmas that surround disability.

I had the opportunity to do just that, thanks to the Aerie Real Me campaign, in 2018. Before I applied for the campaign, I had only ever seen one person in a wheelchair in the media. It was a single picture, and the model was wearing a tracksuit. It was trending on Twitter for all of thirty minutes before something else came up and it was swept under the rug forever. That was it. I had never seen a model in a wheelchair wearing a cute dress, lingerie, or even jeans anywhere in the media. That drove me to apply for this campaign—I wanted to be the person I wanted to see and to be that person for so many other young women like me. After the campaign launched, many girls and women messaged me and thanked me for participating. I had one mom message me saying that her young daughter, who had recently started using a wheelchair, felt so left out and underrepresented while she was flipping through magazines and shopping. When they went to the mall and saw my picture in the store, she practically exploded with happiness and yelled, "MOM! This is it; this is what I was talking about. She looks like me!" Being able to be that for so many people really lit a fire in me to do more of this and to encourage more companies to do it too.

That campaign got the ball rolling. More recently companies like Target, Zappos, and Tommy Hilfiger have released adaptive clothing or used disabled models in their shoots. I even got to be a part of another shoot for LimeLife beauty products as their first disabled model. More and more companies are diversifying their models and realizing that by doing so they are subsequently diversifying their entire brand. They are telling the public that their products are truly for everyone—and meaning it.

Speechless, an ABC sitcom, made giant strides when it came to disability representation. The show navigates the lives of a family with a child who has cerebral palsy and uses a wheelchair, as well as a word sheet and caregiver to speak. The family lives in a severely judgmental and inaccessible world, and the show tackles a lot of problems many school-aged disabled kids face, with grace, humor, and seriousness. The way *Speechless* highlights problems is sharp and poignant without a "this is today's lesson to be learned" kind of cadence. Not only that, but the actor who portrays JJ, the character with cerebral palsy, also has cerebral palsy himself. Seeing a portrayal of disability by someone who is actually disabled and has actually lived the narrative he is acting is such a liberating and educating experience. Not only is his portrayal accurate, but it's a huge step in the media to use a disabled actor for a disabled role.

I HAD NEVER SEEN A MODEL IN A WHEELCHAIR WEARING A CUTE DRESS, LINGERIE, OR EVEN JEANS.

We need to demolish the stereotypes around what disability looks like. But in order to break these stigmas and stereotypes, we have to be willing to actually do the work. Learn what wheelchairs are and how people really use them. Educate yourself on what kinds of disabilities are out there, both invisible and visible. Catch yourself before you judge someone who walks out of their car in a disabled parking space. Ask questions and be open to receiving answers you may have never heard before. Dig into the representations of disability you see in the media and why they might be harmful, especially to the disabled community. Breaking the stigma around the "but you don't look sick" mentality starts and ends with you. So even though I "don't look sick," I am, because it's so much more than looks. Disabilities and chronic illnesses are not, nor have they ever been, a one-size-fits-all style.

FAQS

what is self-care?

Chances are that you've stumbled upon talk about self-care. But self-care is more than a good bubble bath or face mask. Self-care is the radical act of purposefully taking care of your body and your mind.

The current concept of self-care is targeted at middle-class cis white women—because those bodies are easiest for companies to market and sell to. But self-care is for everybody and every body, and it's not about buying or consuming. It's about finding time and allowing space to nurture yourself for you and you alone. It is not an indulgence, nor is it frivolous. Self-care is an essential part of having and operating a human body, and it's a discipline to practice every day.

Self-care is different for everyone, but it might include saying no to things you don't want to do (like going to a party or volunteering for a task that might take time away from sleeping, studying, or enjoying an activity you like more), ensuring you schedule enough sleep every day to function at your best, or moving your body in ways that feel good for the sake of feeling good and not to lose weight or change how you look (whether that involves playing a sport you enjoy, dancing in your room in your underwear, or going for a walk). It might mean filling your social media feeds only with things you like to see and removing any accounts that make you feel bad about yourself.

Baths and face masks and other fun treats can be a part of self-care, but the real work isn't necessarily Instagram-worthy or even all that interesting. Self-care might even be boring. But self-care helps you get up every day, face what's ahead of you, and do so while feeling rested, refreshed, and empowered.

TRIGGER WARNING

BY NAT RAZI

I've read that all hospital waiting rooms are the same—same musty smell, same stiff blue padded seats, same old slightly racist magazines. I don't remember if any of that's true. My theory is no one else does either. The details fuzz, and people just remember the feeling. The same long wait, the same achy spine (maybe that's just me), the same bored scroll through the same five phone apps while the magazines sit unread. Maybe there aren't even magazines. Maybe we just think there ought to be.

(Also the same crying breakdown when you hear for the third time that actually, they don't take your insurance, or actually, your case is closed, or actually . . . And then the same frantic phone calls met with chipper "Your call is important to us!" recordings that lead nowhere. But those stories aren't polite.)

I'm at the hospital for my third independent medical exam, which basically means a doctor looks me over and asks a bunch of questions that all add up to them asking, "The car crash was a year (or two years or three years) ago—do you *really* still need treatment? *Really?*"

This is year three, so my insurance company really wants to stop paying. (They've stopped paying six separate times already, but who's counting?)

Different hospital. Same wait. Same form to fill out. Same panic: What if I say the wrong thing? What if I say my left leg is numb and tingling, and last time I said my right, and I never get coverage again? (Something is always numb and tingling, something is always stabbing, and how am I supposed to rate from one to ten a pain that nestled between my shoulders three years ago and built a nest, a pain that owns more of my body than I ever have?) Same "Twist your head left, right. Lean forward. Lean back."

Pain explodes up my back, and I jolt straight. The doctor laughs. "That was uncomfortable for you, huh?"

Same "Lift your arms." Same tap on my legs. Then I'm gone, a two-minute meeting after a thirty-minute wait. No follow-up questions. Nothing but going back to work and waiting for the doctor to decide what a hundred adults have decided before him: whether what's happening to my body counts as real.

One of my earliest memories, age three or four, is a fight at dinner. My earliest memories are a lot of fights at dinner. Lots of smashed plates in the sink.

In this memory, it's a smashed glass against my head. Dad didn't throw it on purpose, not at me—that matters to me a lot, I think.

I don't remember pain. I do remember a burst of green light fading into a pale blur, probably just milk splashing against my face and hanging off my eyelids.

Years later, I asked my mom if it happened. She said no. Another time she said the glass hit the wall, not my head. Another time, when I remember something else, she said, "But you were wrong about the glass of milk, haha!"

There was a dent in my head for years. You can see it in some pictures. I recall leaning against a mirror, tracing the curve where my skull remembered. When the dent healed, at least too much to be obvious to anything but my fingertips, I mourned. How would I know it was real anymore, with no evidence except my memory and what my nerve endings told me?

Mom likes telling a story about slapping my brother because he bit me. She always tells it as the first time she hit her kids.

I don't remember how many times Mom has hit me. My brain says "not many," but what does it know? I do remember trying to tell her about a book that said you shouldn't hit your kids, and her hitting me and saying how dare I imply that she hits me.

There are a lot of those stories. Not all of them are about denial. Sometimes my dad does say his girlfriend ripped my hair, when he's justifying not wanting me to talk to my stepdad; months later he'll deny it. Sometimes my mom frets that my depression will destroy my entire life, and other times she sneers, "It's always the same excuse, I'm depressed, I'm depressed!"

Sometimes it's about me inflicting my own pain on myself—a scratch here, a slash there, a reminder that I did feel.

Sometimes it's about me trying not to have a body, trying not to eat. Responses from family, most of them the same people: "You look amazing—keep up the good work." "Stop it—you're getting too skinny." "All skin and bones." Years and years later, when I eat enough most of the time, I'll remember and be met with blank looks: "You weren't that thin."

Many stories. They get repetitive.

They're all the same in the end: what you remember isn't real unless the listener wants it to be. The sensations of your body, the marks on your body, aren't real unless the listener wants them to be.

Freshman year of college, a new friend says she worries her roommate's parents may be abusive. I admit I've also experienced abuse. She laughs, throws her arm around me, and says, "You're fine!"

She's known me for a month, but she's already decided she knows more about my life than I do.

Some things get better in college. I learn to eat. I make friends. Smart, funny, interesting friends who are occasionally racist, but at least they're trying.

I run every night. It shuts up some of the clamor in my head. Tires it out, mostly.

On a path I've run a dozen times, something goes wrong. A twist, a blaze of pain, and then I'm on the concrete. (I should say it was cold or hard, should add some nice sensory details, but I don't remember on account of how I'd just fractured my ankle.)

This isn't a story about how people are cruel and don't believe me when I say I hurt. People are wonderful and don't believe me when I say I'm fine. The students who flock to pull me into a chair. The friend who brings me Band-Aids, painkillers, and cookies. Two friends who carry me up the stairs and stick ice on my ankle.

Friends who patiently ignore my chorus of "I'm fine, I'm fine, I'm fine" and leave the pain meds next to me when I insist on sleeping without taking one. I've taught them, in their own way, to ignore what I say about my body.

I don't remember that doctor's visit. I remember arriving to dinner with my foot in a boot, my best friend happily plopping next to me, bracelets jingling, and saying, "Hello, my dear CRIPPLE! You look so nice and CRIPPLED!"

I stood right up and hobbled over to get my own food, ignoring everyone who tried to help.

(This bit is in past tense, because even I look back at it and say, "Wait, really?")

So here's the embarrassing part: I don't stop running. I twist my ankle again and again. I get my other ankle caught between an elliptical's foot pedals, bright bruises blooming like a child scrawled in marker and it leaked, swelling that never quite goes away.

Almost a year later, my ankle an angry red ball, a doctor takes an MRI, and I am utterly shocked to hear my ankle is fractured.

(I remember telling people my ankle was fractured. I just don't remember believing it.)

The doctor says, trying to turn bewilderment into a joke, "It's a shame you didn't wear your boot, huh?"

And what am I supposed to say? I thought I was making the whole thing up?

The car hits us from behind, and my water bottle hits my face. Everything dissolves into green light.

My brother shakes my shoulder, asks if I'm OK. Am I in shock? Do I want an ambulance?

I don't want an ambulance, partially because money, partially because, as always, I think I'm fine.

I'M NOT SAYING I ACTUALLY REMEMBER TO TAKE CARE OF MYSELF ALL THE TIME. BUT I REMEMBER THAT I NEED TO, AT LEAST SOMETIMES.

I'm grateful that to this day, my ankle screams at me for mistakes I made seven years ago, because it reminds me that I need to take care of my back.

I need to let friends help me carry groceries, when I used to be the one stealing other people's bags to carry.

I need to find an identity besides "the one who is always fine, who will take care of you because she has no needs of her own" (the one who is completely delusional but will cook for you!).

I need to lie down for a couple of days after moving apartments, even when my new roommate (the one who said she would totally be down to live with someone disabled, the one who brought me cookies when my ankle broke) is angry and bewildered and asks why I don't get surgery.

I'm not saying I actually remember to take care of myself all the time. But I remember that I need to, at least sometimes.

It's progress.

• • •

I have to call and email my insurance company three times (less than usual) before they send me a simple email with a longer attachment.

The simple email: "The doctor advised that your cervical, thoracic, lumbar, left shoulder, and right shoulder injuries are resolved as related to this claim. Therefore no further treatment is warranted."

The longer attachment spins through lists, my body broken down into numbers, tendon reflexes, range of motion, my name always "the individual" or "the claimant."

Ultimately, the attachment is just as simple as the email. "The claimant's subjective complaints of pain do not match the objective findings. No further treatment would be reasonable or necessary."

I want to end this story on a tidy note. I want to say I learned a lesson, that I take better care of myself and no longer see life as a war between myself and my body. Better yet, I want to say I stormed my insurance company's office or sent a lawyer to do it for me.

And there are much larger stories here. Stories about the crisis of untreated chronic pain. Stories about how we've all learned as a society to turn away from acknowledging the pain of others, especially when they aren't white or male.

But there is no tidy end. It keeps going.

It goes to me waking up in screaming pain most mornings.

It goes to me making an elaborate dinner for friends and then collapsing on the couch while they clean the dishes and occasionally yell at me to get back on the couch and stop trying to clean the dishes.

It goes to one doctor telling me my insurance won't pay for treatment anymore and I should just get exercise, another doctor a year later telling me of course I should keep doing physical therapy, another doctor asking if I've gotten an MRI lately, because this sounds like nerve damage, another doctor telling me maybe it's just the anxiety.

It goes to my body rebelling against me in a thousand tiny ways: hives all over, constant gas that fizzes and pops under a stethoscope (much to my relief, because what if I was making it up?).

It goes to a different insurance company, a different hospital room, same wait, same form, same questions.

Yes, it happened in 2016.

Yes, I'm still seeking treatment.

Yes, I'm sure it hurts.

MAYBE IT'S MAYBELLINE, OR MAYBE IT'S REALLY NOT YOUR BUSINESS

BY ROSHANI CHOKSHI

I've just emerged from putting the finishing touches of makeup on for date night. When I get to the foyer, I tilt my chin up, don my best approximation of an insouciant moue, and say, "OK. Now I'm ready."

My fiancé looks at me. To be beheld by someone who loves you can transmute the blood in your veins, and right now, I feel a rush of fizzing champagne.

"Notice anything different?" I ask.

Too late, I realize this registers to him as a trap question. Alarm blares in his eyes as he abruptly shuts off the mental shuffle of whatever Instagram memes he was scrolling through moments ago and starts mentally rummaging through the day's conversations.

"No?" he says almost guiltily before adding a safe closer: "You always look beautiful."

I glance in the mirror. Tonight, I've dabbed a pearlescent highlighter on the Cupid's bow of my lips and the crescents along my cheekbones. When I turn my face, I catch an almost fae-like shimmer by my temples. It struck me as coquettish—a detail that appears and disappears in a slant of light. I tell him what I added, demonstrating the shimmer by turning my head this way and that.

"Oh," he says before frowning. "I can't really tell the difference."

"Ah, but I *know* the difference," I say, smiling as I take his arm.

Makeup, for me, is less about what others perceive and more about what I wish to project. It's an art form, an act of ritual, a semblance of armor even.

When I was growing up, my mother wore little makeup. Her only cosmetic ritual—if it can be called that—was cold cream and Noxzema, and those faintly mentholated bedtime kisses became a background fragrance to my childhood. In the morning, Mom swabbed on her favorite toner and SPF and went about her day. But on special occasions, she would open up a wicker basket that she kept on her counter and take out a shiny black tube of lipstick. I adored the waxen rose smell of her lipstick, the way her repeated use had changed the pillar of color, so that it dipped into a mauve crescent. Mom would draw her lipstick on like a heart, filling both halves of her upper lip before finishing the bottom lip in one smooth swipe. She would blot once with a tissue, then dust powder over her face. I loved to watch her fluff her hair once, her eyebrows arched slightly as she drew back, an imperial aura haloing her silhouette. My mother has always been powerful, but that swipe of lipstick and dust of powder lent her a sheen of self-awareness. She was powerful, and she wanted you to know that *she* knew it too.

Naturally, I wanted a taste of what that felt like.

In sixth grade, I crept into my parents' bathroom and furtively dabbed on my mom's lipstick (a full, pressed swipe was far too bold and unwieldy). When I looked in the mirror, I mimicked her eyebrow arch and chin tilt, and I. Felt. *Fearsome.* I didn't even notice that I'd smudged the lipstick outside of the lip line. And I definitely couldn't tell that it'd caught on my snaggletooth and braces . . . until, of course, I got to school. I don't know what I expected.

Maybe too many Bollywood movies or lazy rom-coms in which the heroine takes down her hair and causes a seismic shift in the universe had trained my soul to think how that *one* lipsticked smile would make the entire room break into choreographed dancing. When I walked into class, I grinned widely at my crush. I braced myself for a rain of silvery confetti. A sudden bloom of awareness behind his eyes.

Instead, he took one look at my blood-claggy teeth and recoiled like I'd arrived to homeroom waving a vial of smallpox.

After that, I shoved the lipstick back into the depths of Mom's makeup basket, furious with its betrayal.

I didn't mess with makeup after that. I didn't trust it. Whatever power it had, it clearly had no interest in working for me.

I didn't reach for makeup again until I was in high school. My dad wouldn't let me wear contact lenses; I still had braces; and to better frame my mouth of metal, I unwillingly sported a dusting of facial hair. It would be a kindness to call it a Groucho Marx aesthetic. In certain lights, I was convinced it looked like I'd taken in a homeless badger and allowed it to live right beneath my nose.

Alas.

My best friend proposed a solution: Nair, a depilatory cream and darling of the early '00s. *What could go wrong?* proclaimed the advertisements. Indeed.

A few days before the homecoming dance, I perched on her toilet seat, nose wrinkling from the corpse reek of the product as she slathered it over my upper lip.

"Now we wait eight minutes," she said.

Eight minutes seemed like a longish time, so we puttered around her house, annoyed the cats, scavenged through her fridge, and got distracted by a rerun of *Totally Spies!* By then, I'd gotten used to the reek of Nair, and I remembered it was there only when I felt a faint stinging sensation.

"Do you think we should wash this stuff off now?" I asked her.

"Hmm?" she said distractedly. Then she looked at my face: "Shit."

When I slunk back home, I sported swatches of peeling, raw skin below my nose. I wanted to burst into flames. Even worse, my parents were *furious*.

My dad, who lives for ominous pronouncements, declared that I would be permanently scarred. I cried for hours before walking to the nearby pharmacy, desperate for a solution. Inside I was met with a spectrum of concealers, a rainbow of pristine skin bearing names like "Honey," "Caramel," "Toast," and "Café au Lait." It was a lexicon of camouflage, and I wanted to hide so badly. I grabbed a shade that I thought matched my face, got home, and dabbed it over my bruised skin. It was a bit cakey, a bit yellow tinged, and the more it was exposed to light, the more it oxidized. I saw all that, sure, but what I *didn't* see was a scabbed-over mustache.

That was the start of my new relationship with makeup. It wasn't just a swipe of self-aware power. It could be expression too. If I wished to hide something, I could. If I wanted to look bright, I could. Dark, I could. It was potential, and my face was a canvas.

Those early years with makeup summoned a strange tension. There were days when I felt like my cystic acne and terrible scars meant that I shouldn't even walk into my parents' kitchen without a layer of foundation, concealer, and powder. If I went to a party and felt beautiful, all those compliments melted from me the moment I washed my face and saw what lay underneath. A sort of dysmorphia set in, where who I was felt inextricable from what I looked like.

I think a large part of that unease with my own face came from not knowing what I was *supposed* to look like.

I grew up wanting to look like the beauties from my favorite books or the shows around me: Alanna the Lioness, Fleur Delacour, Sailor Moon, Lizzie McGuire. Girls with uncomplicated names and candlelight hair, gemstone eyes, and milk skin. It wasn't until I graduated high school that interest shifted a little. The Kardashians ushered an era of exoticizing the ethnically ambiguous, the girls whose bloodlines showed no particular allegiance and celebrated the in-between.

I'd always struggled with how to be both Filipina and Indian. If I was half of each, could I still wholly belong to both? I thought my face would decide for me, but a touch more eyeliner there, a straighter hairstyle here, and, well, I could slip between realms of belonging or eschew them both entirely.

> # LEARNING ABOUT MAKEUP BECAME A CELEBRATION OF SELF.

At that point, makeup became a language of control. "Indian girls shouldn't look too tan. Stay fair," counseled one aunt. So I bought bronzer and self-tanner. "Asian girls shouldn't wear too much eyeliner. It makes their eyes look small." So I became a raccoon impersonator.

As I grew older, time became crueler in some ways but kinder in others. Its best kindness to me was that I grew accustomed to myself. At a certain point, it became exhausting to exceed or defy anyone else's expectations of me, so I endeavored to meet my own. I reached for makeup to enhance what I loved about my features, rather than to transform what I disliked. Makeup was no longer about what I couldn't control, but about what I wanted to craft . . . *for fun*. For *me*. It was a new stage in my relationship with makeup, and all I had to do was, well, wait to grow up a bit.

Learning about makeup became a celebration of self. I learned the difference between red lipsticks with blue undertones and red lipsticks with clementine souls and chose what fit me best based on the hue of the veins on my wrist. I learned how to open up my eyes with shadows that smoked along the corners rather than dusting the entire surface. I learned that experimenting with looks was an act of artistic expression.

Even now, I love to sink deeper into the mind-set of a character I'm writing by changing up my makeup look to match them. When my brain looks like a ziggurat of adverbs and descriptions of a love interest's eyes, and the plot demands a bloody sacrifice before it moves an inch further, I swipe on red lipstick, glare at my laptop, and plunge back into the book.

These days, I love taking off my makeup almost as much as I love putting it on. I live for the ritual of returning to bareness—the cotton pads like flattened moons, soap lather squishing between fingers, glossy creams sinking into my skin. The repetitive motions take the day away. If I get a bad review, it's swiped off with the concealer. If I regret cruel words I let slip, a clean lip is a clean slate to do better.

Sometimes I hear, "Oh, but you don't need makeup." Other times I hear, "Do you need to wear *that* much?" Need is a strange condition. As an artist, I need an outlet for expression. Sometimes I need armor and sometimes I need invisibility. Those needs don't negate my self-worth or sense of self. Rather, they're things I do for myself that no one need notice. There may be days when no one else around me can tell what difference I've added or subtracted, but it doesn't matter.

Because I know.

And I'm the only one who needs to know.

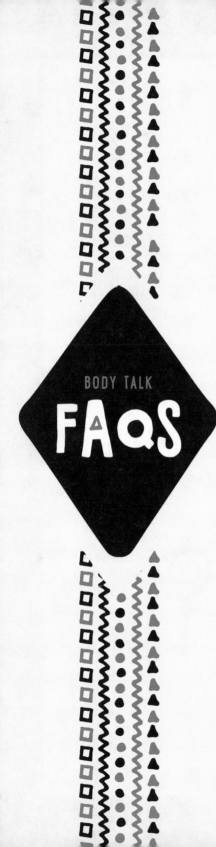

BODY TALK
FAQS

How important is sleep?

Human bodies need sleep. It's where some of the most important growth happens. The challenge is, of course, that the world doesn't operate on the best schedule for allowing your body to sleep. Teens need eight to ten hours of sleep every night, but because of changes in hormones and circadian rhythms, you might not be able to fall asleep until late at night. That means waking up early for school can be challenging. And when your body doesn't get enough sleep, it can impact everything from your cognitive function to the way your skin looks. You might not be able to concentrate, and you might find yourself quick to get angry.

One of the best ways to ensure you're getting enough sleep is to establish a routine by going to bed at the same time every night and waking up at the same time every morning. It can be tempting to sleep in on weekends, but if you go to bed and wake up around the same time every day, your body will know when to shut down and wake up in a healthy pattern. Other ways to help get good sleep include routines that tell your body it's time to unwind, like taking a shower or bath before getting into bed, turning off all screens an hour before you want to fall asleep, writing out a to-do list for the next day, journaling, doing gentle stretches, or anything else that helps you relax. Try not to rely on caffeine or energy supplements in the evening, and if you choose to take a nap during the day, limit it to about twenty minutes and make sure it's not too close to your normal bedtime.

If you struggle with sleeping for long periods of time, it's OK to see your doctor about it. There are many reasons why you may be unable to sleep, and there are many treatments that can help.

WHAT'S THE DEAL WITH HORMONES?

BY ALICIA LUTES

For all the things your hormones affect and control in your body, it's sort of wild we don't talk about them more. Maybe it's because they're so hard to pin down—your responses and reactions are personal, depending on your family history as well as other external forces. Hormones show you just how truly connected every part of our bodies really are.

I know this because as a teenager, I was tested for Cushing's disease, a rare condition in which your pituitary gland overproduces the hormones ACTH and cortisol (ACTH is the hormone that regulates cortisol production). Weight that feels impossible to lose is one of several symptoms of the disease. Even though I tried to shrug the diagnosis off, like any other teen would, learning about the interconnectedness of my hormones ultimately paved the way to understanding my physical and mental health as an adult. So I thought, who better to ask about hormones than the woman who helped me understand them when I was sixteen? Thankfully, Dr. Kai Yang, an adult endocrinologist affiliated with Yale University, along with Dr. Susan Boulware, a pediatric endocrinologist and assistant professor at Yale, was more than happy to answer my questions and hopefully help all of you to understand your hormones, too.

All right, Dr. Yang, lay it on me: What are hormones, and where do they come from?

So, hormones are proteins or substances made by glands. They travel through the body—usually in the bloodstream—to other organs and regulate many things. For instance, the pancreas makes insulin, which "talks to" several tissues and causes those tissues to either take in glucose (sugar) or remove sugar from the bloodstream. Your thyroid makes hormones that control temperature regulation, metabolism, regulation of periods—all that stuff. And one of the most important organs is the pituitary gland, located at the base of your brain. An extremely tiny gland, it regulates many of your organs that affect how you grow and the production of breast milk, and it also controls the adrenal glands, the ovaries, and the testicles in order to make the sex hormones (your estrogens and testosterone).

Why are hormones so important but so hard to track or talk about?

Hormones affect a lot of organ systems, depending on when and how much are produced, making their timing important for puberty, the time when hormones start being produced in your body. This also means young adults are very affected by their endocrine systems, as the normal cycles of your body are being created at this stage. Glands that produce hormones do so in a very controlled, cyclical fashion, which means they may be higher in the morning and lower in the afternoon. Because of this variation, when we draw labs, we get only a snapshot of what someone's levels are—we can't tell if the timing is off or if the hormones are going up and down a lot. Since it's hard to "see" what the hormones are doing all the time, this may be why people don't talk about them much. It's difficult to pinpoint which hormone is fluctuating and whether it is the cause of certain symptoms.

Sounds like a properly functioning hormonal system is pretty important for our development!

Absolutely. Hormones affect many different systems, so if the levels are too high or too low or what we call dysregulated (too much or too little of a response), you could feel some symptoms. Hormonal issues are more likely to affect physical health than mental health, but this may be because the effects on physical health have been studied more—and are easier to sort out—than mental health. If one doesn't feel well physically, that can affect how you feel mentally.

So hormones can affect your mental health and general mood?

Some hormonal fluctuations, like thyroid hormone fluctuations, can definitely affect your mood. Or cortisol, which is often called the stress hormone. Since hormones are cyclical, a person's cortisol level is higher in the morning and lower in the afternoon. So if the hormonal level is high all the time, that would definitely create issues both physically and mentally. Another good example of this is the hormones that regulate periods. The pituitary gland produces hormones that regulate estrogen and progesterone production, and the pulsatility (velocity) of these signals can cause different levels of estrogen to be secreted at different times. The cyclical nature of these hormones' production is the reason people with internal reproductive systems have periods. The hormonal level could also be controlled by other, external factors, such as severe weight loss or gain, medications, drugs, alcohol use, inadequate sleep or nutrition, etc.

All this hormone talk makes me wonder how trans and nonbinary kids' hormones might be playing into things.

You should talk to Susan Boulware, a pediatric endocrinologist here at Yale.

Great idea. Hi, Dr. Boulware! Thanks for speaking with me about this. Is there anything important to consider when it comes to trans and nonbinary kids going through puberty or dealing with their own hormones?

When trans and nonbinary kids hit puberty, they're really questioning their body, so if at puberty they have to proceed with the gender they were assigned at birth, it can be a very discordant process. Everybody, even cisgender kids, has a hard time going through puberty, but it's really compounded for non-cisgender kids because their bodies are changing and they're really feeling different from where their body is going. It's hard to ascribe specific feelings, specific behaviors, and specific experiences to a specific hormone, because everybody makes both testosterone and estrogen, so the irritability and emotionality we all experience is not that different or due to gender. There is a decrease in anxiety when we give young trans and nonbinary people the hormone blockers, and a decrease in psychological distress, but there's not enough data out there to say whether that is resulting from or relational to being placed on the blockers. It's reassuring to be told some of what you're feeling is due to changes in hormones in your body.

Thanks, Dr. Boulware! That was so helpful. Dr. Yang, now I have to ask you about how hormones might affect our interpersonal bonds and/or gender expression.

Well, while I personally do not necessarily subscribe to ideas about oxytocin affecting your interpersonal bonds, there is definitely a suggestion that hormones can affect people's attractions, identity, and gender. For instance, girls who have congenital adrenal hyperplasia (a very complex disorder) may experience more gender differences than those without the disorder. And testosterone is present in and affects both male and female patients. In fact, sometimes gynecologists give low doses of testosterone to postmenopausal people to help with libido—the body is an amazing thing! Think about it: if you don't drink enough water or get enough sleep, or if you eat junk food, your body just adapts, and you don't even know that all this stuff is going on to keep it that way. Your body is working so hard every day to keep you in equilibrium. The most important thing we can do to treat our bodies right is to avoid abusing substances that are toxic, keep up with proper nutrition habits, try to get enough sleep, etc.

But how can you keep track of all the ways in which how we live, what we eat, and the stress we encounter can affect our hormones when it seems so overwhelmingly interconnected?

Well, the problem is that the body can't talk to you and say, "Hey, you aren't getting enough sleep, so you're exhausted, and drinking energy drinks to stay awake is why you're jittery and anxious all the time!" Keeping your body healthy can be difficult because you have to interpret the symptoms and figure out—alongside your doctors—what you are doing that might not be good for your body. And to complicate matters, everyone is different. So let's say a lot of people in your family have diabetes because your family tends to have pancreases that aren't able to make a lot of insulin. If you challenge your body with things that challenge insulin function (like eating too many sugary treats), eventually your pancreas might "poop out," so to speak, and you might end up with insulin resistance or eventually diabetes. It's all about listening to your body and talking to medical professionals; it's their job, and they're here to help!

As someone who's been overweight for most of her life, I wonder whether there's a bigger connection between hormones and weight than maybe we originally thought. Where do you land on the matter?

Thyroid hormones affect metabolism, so the standard thought is that high levels of these hormones in your body cause weight loss, and low levels cause weight gain. While in general this is true, it can be different for everyone. Part of this variability has to do with the hormones that bind to receptors in different tissues—some people may be very sensitive to the different binding characteristics and thus may experience different effects for the same hormonal levels. So your body may respond in a completely different way to the same levels of hormones as mine does. Plus, hormones are cyclical, and just drawing a level here or there can be misleading!

Gosh, it can be really confusing to try to make sense of your hormones.

IT'S GOOD TO FIND OUT WHAT IS NOT NORMAL, BUT REMEMBER, EVERY BODY IS DIFFERENT!

That is why I think hormones seem like such a mysterious entity. There can be a lot of variability in the onset of puberty, based on nutritional and environmental factors, family history, and so forth. So a lot of this variability is what we call physiologic, or normal. It's good to find out what is not normal, but remember, every body is different!

Learning more about your hormones isn't some sort of one-size-fits-all explainer for your body's specific behaviors. But it *is* like unlocking the super-secret elixir of life that makes you, well, you! And in ways you may not realize! Unlike other parts of your body, where things can be a bit more black and white, hormones are different for everybody, and how yours respond to things can be unique to you. It's easy, sometimes, to listen blindly to those we think know better, but if anything, hormones' uniqueness to our own systems is a great reminder to trust your gut when it comes to what you're feeling inside your own body.

FART FROM THE MADDING CROWD

BY KARA THOMAS

Warning: there will be fart jokes. Probably a lot of them. So if that's not your thing, clear out now.

I was away for my first year of college, five hours from home, when the symptoms started. Terrible, gut-twisting pain in the middle of the night. Running to the bathroom after every meal. And most embarrassingly, gas that could clear the savanna like Pumbaa's. Not exactly an ideal situation for me or my roommate.

A strange gastrointestinal illness didn't factor into my freshman-year plans. I wrote the symptoms off as the result of stress, since I had plenty to be stressed about—I hated living in a city, and my dream school was looking more and more like an expensive mistake each day. I stubbornly avoided seeing a doctor for months, until I arrived home for the summer. I was bounced from bored specialist to bored specialist (one politely asked if stress over college might be making me sick) until one shrugged and tossed a diagnosis of irritable bowel syndrome at me. I was too embarrassed to tell friends what was wrong. It even sounded ridiculous: *I have irritable bowels.* I imagined my intestines raging at me every time I had the audacity to eat: *Bitch, are we really doing this again?* The pills I was supposed to take before eating did nothing to alleviate my symptoms. By that point I had already transferred to my local state university for my second year of college, knowing I couldn't possibly go away for school again as sick as I was, let alone to a school that was making me miserable.

All the while, my symptoms worsened. The pain moved into my back, and the bathroom trips increased. More doctors, more horse-pill antibiotics I had to choke down with yogurt. Antibiotics with diarrhea as a side effect—what the hell was the point, then? I had just accepted my new hellish reality when I arrived home from my job at a deli and curled into a ball on my bathroom floor from the abdominal pain. My dad took me to the emergency room, where in triage my temperature clocked in at 104 and my blood count was somewhere in the range of *how are you alive?* I still remember the doctor strolling into the room, looking at the cup of urine on my bedside table, and proclaiming, "That is *ridiculously* infected." I wanted to hug him. How low had I sunk that an off-hand comment about my pee had finally made me feel seen? Finally, a doctor was taking me seriously and promising not to send me home until we knew what was wrong.

That doctor admitted me, and what transpired over the next week was like a super-low-drama episode of *House*. I had a kidney infection. I was so anemic I needed a blood transfusion. My veins became so battered that after an hour of struggling, the nurse had to put the needle for said transfusion in my hand. Someone else's blood going into my veins burned so badly that I asked her if my parents could stay with me, even though visiting hours were over. I caught her roll her eyes as she left the room; that's what finally unglued me and made me break down into sobs. A nurse I'd never see again judging me for being a big baby.

A slew of tests, a parade of doctors, but no one could conclusively say what was wrong with me until after the big kahuna of tests: a colonoscopy. Afterward, the gastroenterologist sat my parents down and told the three of us that it looked like Crohn's disease. My dad immediately went pale and slumped out of his chair. (My parents have always had a penchant for drama. It's true what they say about having only one kid: you never shed the new-parent neurosis, even when your kid is nineteen.)

"Please get a grip," I told him. "It's not cancer."

The doctor, who is still my ride-or-die ten years later, looked at my dad. "Crohn's is actually very manageable."

My dad's response was swift. "My coworker's son has Crohn's. His gas smells so bad he can never leave the house."

Suffice it to say, I've been able to leave the house since my diagnosis. But navigating everything that comes with it has been more complicated.

The quick and dirty on Crohn's: it's an inflammatory bowel disease that causes nausea, vomiting, abdominal pain, and diarrhea. The exact cause is unknown, but since it's an autoimmune disease, genetics could play a role. There's no cure. During a bad flare, I almost always wind up in the emergency room, vomiting *Exorcist*-style and in the fetal position from pain. I manage my symptoms with an intense medication every eight weeks that takes three hours to administer via IV at the hospital. The medication costs $18,000 per treatment; if I didn't have insurance, I don't know what I'd do. Die, I guess? No, Crohn's is rarely fatal. But life would be unbearably miserable if I left my condition untreated.

It took me seven years to find a medication regimen that worked for me—I tried every treatment, from injections to steroids, from low-dose chemotherapy pills to no treatment at all. But now, even the bad days are survivable, thanks to my obscenely expensive wonder drug. When I am grumbling over not being able to have that second glass of wine because I know it will make me sick, I remind myself that I'm lucky. My intestines haven't had to be diced up, the inflamed pieces removed like sashimi. I don't have to crap into a bag. People I've known for years don't even realize I have a chronic disease, and that's how I've always preferred it. No, we don't need to talk about my inflamed bowels, just like we don't need to talk about your healthy bowels. Unless you really want to.

But living with an invisible illness is a double-edged sword. As much as I like being treated like a healthy person, there are times when I need people to remember I am not a 100-percent-healthy person. In my experience, you can't have it both ways. There are days when my body cannot get its shit together (literally) and I have to yo-yo between the bathroom and my bed. Murphy's Law of Inflammatory Bowel Disease states that my stomach must always act up at the worst possible moments. As I'm

LIVING WITH AN INVISIBLE ILLNESS IS A DOUBLE-EDGED SWORD.

boarding an airplane. Right before an important work phone call. My second year of college, I missed a final exam because I was so sick I didn't even remember I had a test that day. Begging that professor not to fail me was one of the most demoralizing things I've ever had to do. She icily agreed to let me take the exam only after I produced a doctor's note. I knew what she was thinking: I'd sat in her class all semester and never once even looked sick. Now I was playing the Crohn's card—I wanted special treatment, even though she had a zero-tolerance policy about makeups on the final.

The screwed-up thing is that all these years later, I still feel like I cheated my way out of failing that exam.

Living with my condition has made me hyperaware of the narrative around illness, or more specifically, the pain that accompanies many chronic illnesses. You're weak if you can't deal with pain, and you're some sort of champion if you can. If the moral judgment surrounding coping with pain wasn't evident from my trips to the hospital over the years, having a baby drove home the point. *Are you doing it all natural, or are you getting an epidural?* is everyone's way of asking, *Can you deal with the pain?* (If you must know, no, I could not, and I took every drug they offered me.)

Before I gave birth, a friend casually said that she was surprised I was worried about labor pains after dealing with Crohn's disease for so long. I know she didn't mean it to be cruel, but all I heard was *Shouldn't you be used to this by now?* I am used to comments and advice from well-meaning people. Part of the reason I don't advertise my illness is because there are *too many* well-meaning people who are happy to share opinions on something they don't really know much about. *Have you tried managing your diet?* No, I have not tried healing my incurable disease with boiled roots and dandelion tea, but thanks for the suggestion. *What about exercise?* I know you think running and yoga can cure everything, Carol, but there are days I can't even walk upright. And then there are the people obsessed with noticing my weight loss and complimenting me on it—I wasn't able to eat for a week because of a flare, but sure, I guess I do look "great."

I don't expect people to be 100 percent literate in How to Talk to Someone with Crohn's. But if there's any perspective I've gained from my own experience, it's that people are obsessed with commenting on bodies. Specifically, women's bodies. The size of them, what we put into them, what comes out of them. Obsessed, yes, but repulsed at the same time. Poop and farts are taboo. I've wrestled with the stigma of having an inflammatory bowel disease for years; why would I want to talk about something so gross? Why would anyone want to hear about it?

I can only hope that by sharing my experience, I might help someone else feel less alone. Someone who is struggling with the shame might be encouraged to open up; someone who is too sick to see hope for the future might realize a normal life with Crohn's is possible.

My "normal life" is not ideal. The uncertainty sucks; my wonder drug has serious drawbacks, including a weakened immune system and an increased risk for developing lymphoma in the future. Someday, maybe there will be a cure for Crohn's. Until then, I'll continue to make jokes. It might seem glib to joke about something so serious, but my dad likes to say if you can't laugh at something shitty, you'll cry.

Recently, I found myself in a HomeGoods parking lot, covered in my son's poop after he decided to blow out his diaper in the middle of a shopping trip.

Somehow, he had managed to get feces in both his hair and mine, and all I could think was *Goddamn it, I just wanted to get some place mats.* When I realized I hadn't packed a spare outfit for him, I burst into tears. Then the sight of him in his car seat, stark nude except for a diaper, sent me into hysterical laughter.

It's true that life can be shitty, and if you can't laugh at it, you'll cry. But I've found that it's more than fine to do both at the same time.

OUR WHOLE SELVES

OUR BODIES ARE INCREDIBLE MACHINES,

and whether or not they're able to function the way we wish they would all the time, we each only ever get one. Its form may change or shift. It may add pounds or various hardware to make it more mobile. But in the end, each person has only one body.

This section looks at how and where our bodies offer us insight into the greater parts of who we are, both on the inside and in the world at large. This is about sharing laughs, about sharing cringey experiences, about leaning into loving the things that make our bodies—us!—what we are.

BODY POSITIVE

BY ALY RAISMAN

Needham, Massachusetts
Spring 2015

I was eating lunch at home, covered in chalk from training (as usual), when the phone rang.

"We've been in talks with ESPN to feature you in their Body Issue," a member of the Octagon team [my management] informed me.

The news threw me for a loop. The Body Issue was one of *ESPN The Magazine*'s most popular editions—and there was one big reason why.

"Naked, you mean?" I said nervously.

"That's the idea," he responded.

"Do I get approval of the photos?" I asked.

"No, you don't." That wasn't what I had hoped to hear. In my endorsement deals, there's always a line in my contract that says I have approval over the images. With magazines, that isn't the case. Not having control over the images was all the more nerve-wracking when we were talking about naked photos (even if they'd ensure that no private parts were visible).

"Can I think about it for a while?" I said.

When we hung up, I sat back, chewing thoughtfully. I was not at all sure I felt comfortable about posing naked. I pictured myself typing my name into Google, knowing that naked photos of me had been published—and there was nothing I could do if I didn't like what I saw. I also wondered how the people I knew would react. My coaches, for example. Or Martha [Karolyi]. What would they think?

I thought about calling back immediately and saying no thanks, but something held me back. I had learned the importance of taking some time before making a big decision. Sometimes sitting back and reflecting for a while can make you see things in a whole new light.

I talked it over with my parents, who I was half expecting to quash the idea immediately. But to my surprise, they agreed with me that it was a great opportunity, and saw that it could be an empowering, confidence-building moment. After all, my parents had always taught me to love myself.

"We'll support you no matter what you decide," Mom said. "But you shouldn't say no just because you're afraid that someone won't approve of it."

[My brother] Brett was far less enthusiastic. "You're going to pose naked for a magazine?" he said, horrified. "Do you realize what my friends are going to say when they see this? I'll never hear the end of it!"

My sisters were divided. "If that's what you want to do, you should do it," Chloe said, shrugging.

"But why would you want to?" Maddie wanted to know.

I mulled Maddie's question over while driving to practice that evening. While chalking up for bars. While doing crunches. While stretching.

If I were a man, this would be no big deal, I told myself. Men pose for these things all the time. *Why is it different because I'm a woman?*

I'd come to realize that girls and women face lots of pressure from society about their bodies. Instead of feeling good about the wonderful things about them, they are taught to dislike what makes them stand out. I thought about my own experiences in school, when boys had made fun of me for being muscular (as if that was anything but rad!). Girls who had filled out early had teased me for not developing at the same rate. All along, others who I'd thought were "perfect" confessed to feeling ashamed of their bodies. I shook my head. *Why do we all feel this way?* I wondered.

Even in sports, I realized the toughest female athletes are not always given the respect they deserve. On my beloved 1996 Olympic tape, the women who competed in Atlanta were referred to as "little girls" and their difficult floor routines characterized as "dancing."

I heard an actress who had been raped say that when she shared her story, people sometimes asked, "What were you wearing?" As though wearing a sexy outfit gave a man the right to disrespect her. As though it was her fault she had been attacked.

It made me mad. I realized that I wanted to tell people that everyone deserves respect, regardless of their body type or what they were (or weren't) wearing. We should all be able to express ourselves in any way we want, without judgment, no matter what our gender.

Sometimes, if you want to take a stand about something, you have to do something a bit controversial, I figured. If proudly displaying my muscular body helped one person feel good about theirs, I thought, it's worth it. And if seeing my photos and reading the accompanying interview could help teach the next generation to love themselves and their bodies—a task made difficult by social media—all the better.

Plus, I was tired of being afraid of what other people thought of me. I was used to being judged in competitions, which spilled over into worry that people were judging me in other ways, and now into concern that people would judge my naked body. As a result, there had been so many years when I had thought my body was too muscular, too this, not enough that. But I had worked my whole life to look the way I did, and I was through letting anyone make me ashamed of my body. I was now twenty years old, and training for a second Olympics had made me appreciate my body like never before. Everyone's body deserves to be celebrated. Everyone deserves to feel proud of who they are.

I had always weighed decisions by asking myself "What will everyone else think?" first and "What do I want to do?" second. It was time to listen to my voice above the others.

I called Octagon back the next day. When I spoke, my voice was firm.

"I'll do it," I said.

EVERYONE'S BODY DESERVES TO BE CELEBRATED. EVERYONE DESERVES TO FEEL PROUD OF WHO THEY ARE.

The crew had drawn two canvas curtains across the windows of a Newton [Massachusetts] studio and created a small alcove for hair and makeup. A white terrycloth bathrobe with the words "ESPN Body Issue" embroidered on the back in red was waiting for me. I slipped it on, along with ESPN slippers (so that my socks wouldn't leave imprints on my ankles), and sat in the makeup chair as the makeup artist dusted a light powder over my face, with straightened hair to add some drama.

We had a few phone calls with the ESPN team beforehand to discuss options that would make the shoot unique and the images artistic. Two giant light fixtures cast a soft white glow on the gymnastics equipment set up around the studio. From a distance, my mom and my aunt Jessica stood and took in the scene. Jessica had never been to one of my photo shoots before. "You really picked an interesting one to come to!" I said, laughing.

When the moment came to begin, I took a deep breath and dropped the robe, handing it to an ESPN assistant. For five minutes, I felt nervous, and then I forgot I was naked, just as the staff on the shoot had reassured me I would. Their support and professionalism made me feel completely confident.

I clicked with the photographer, Mark Seliger, right away. We were bouncing ideas off each other and I made the final decisions about the poses. Each was meant to highlight the beauty and power of the human form. Throughout the shoot, I felt empowered and strong.

A few months later, I was at July camp when I saw a tweet from *People* magazine and my heart started thudding in my chest. "Click here to see Aly Raisman naked," the tweet started. Being at the ranch where the cell and internet service was weak, of course the link took forever to load.

When it finally came up, I looked at the site for just a few seconds and closed it so I wouldn't be tempted to pick myself apart. Later, when I saw the photos in print, I felt proud. I was truly happy about the way I looked. And I hoped this would mark a new chapter for me, where I could move forward knowing that confidence has to come from within.

This piece was previously published in Fierce *by Aly Raisman.*

ODE TO A SPIT CUP

BY ALICE WONG

Spit. Drool. Saliva. Our bodies secrete this clear liquid, up to one or two liters, every day. Depending on hydration, diet, medication, and other factors, saliva can be watery, sticky, bubbly, and infused with whatever is in your mouth at the moment. Bodily fluids can be endlessly fascinating, and following an increased difficulty swallowing, I developed a brand-new respect for saliva.

I was born with a neuromuscular disability, which means that all my muscles progressively weaken. Over time, my body's trajectory is always headed downward, its pace unknown. I stopped walking at about the age of seven, and at fourteen my severe scoliosis required a spinal-fusion surgery. Complications after this surgery added new concerns on top of lack of mobility. As my diaphragm muscles weakened, sleeping and breathing became major issues. I did breathing treatments with a nebulizer and an intermittent positive pressure breathing machine, used oxygen at night, and benefited from other interventions until I developed respiratory failure at eighteen. Since I had severe sleep apnea, I needed to sleep with a BiPAP machine at night or else I could die from respiratory failure.

Fast-forward to today, and I'm a person who uses a BiPAP machine full-time. I now consider my power chair and BiPAP machine to be extensions of my body. They're part of my personal space and sense of self. And in the last few years, I gained another bodily extension: my spit cup.

What is a spit cup? Very simply, it's a paper cup I keep nearby so I can spit out my saliva rather than swallow it.

I can still swallow, but it's actually quite tiring over an entire day. The spit cup provides a shortcut, as well as a way to preempt possible aspiration in case things go down the wrong pipe. My spit cup has become my new friend, a brilliant adaptation, and a source of wonderment.

I'm now hyperaware of two interconnected bodily functions: breathing and swallowing. Previously, breathing was the top priority. I continue to fear the tremendous toll on my body whenever I catch a flu or cold and try to cough out my secretions. I still worry about the amount of battery life on my BiPAP machine when I am out for a long time or during a power outage. Whenever I eat a full meal, I cannot talk or breathe comfortably. Through all these concerns and changes, I adapted. I reduced my exposure to crowds during flu season. When I started to need BiPAP for the entire day, I got the machine connected to my wheelchair battery for extended life. I changed my diet and focused on high-fat, high-protein meals to make the most out of every bite. I scheduled smaller meals and snacks to lessen the feeling of distension.

When I wear my BiPAP during the day, the machine produces a set number of breaths per minute. These breaths are not initiated by me; my rhythm is dictated by the machine. When I talk, there are "unnatural" pauses because of the incoming breaths. Swallowing becomes complicated when you're working on a machine's timetable. I can't just swallow my saliva, or anything else, whenever I want—I have to time it right after a breath. Sometimes a breath happens midswallow, which causes me to panic and choke. The BiPAP has given me an incredible amount of respiratory support, and I know my life span and the ability to conserve my energy have increased because of it. But since I cannot separate the machine from my body, I have to work within this technical ecosystem as conditions evolve and shift.

Maintaining the ability to breathe had been the top priority. But within the last five years, swallowing became the second major function to reshape the direction and orientation of my world. Can you imagine how many times humans swallow food, liquids, or saliva in a twenty-four-hour period? Think about the nerves and muscles involved in chewing, swallowing, and breathing, the kinds of things that, for most people, happen almost effortlessly.

I used to choke on the simplest things: a drink, a tiny bit of saliva, food if I was laughing while eating. For me, aspirating creates a reaction that feels like a life-or-death situation. I will frantically try to breathe, but air can't come in. My eyes bulge and tear up, my face becomes flushed, and I struggle to cough, clawing and swiping at my mortality. Everything tenses up, and then it slowly clears as the trachea relaxes and opens up again. By then, my face is a wet soggy mess, my breaths ragged and irregular, but I'm filled with relief to be alive.

Is saliva my enemy? I don't think so. It's always present, and it's an important part of the digestion process. Aspiration shocks my system, but it reminds me of the frailty of life and human vulnerability. Rather than hating and fighting it, or taking medications to reduce it, or being depressed about my growing difficulties with yet another major bodily function, I started using a spit cup as a DIY hedge against frequent choking. It gives my esophagus muscles a break, however slight. The spit cup was a gift to myself, a literal life hack.

I learned how to present myself and move through spaces with this new accessory. By our culture's standards, saliva is seen as gross and messy outside of the body. Spitting and drooling in public is gauche. It's also an act that is infantilized, making it easy to feel shame and to be hurt by the internalized ableism. I had to work through my self-consciousness, holding the cup to the side, handling it carefully, discreetly spitting into it when out with friends. I worried about accidental spillage (and yes, it's happened a few times) and people staring or looking at the cup's contents. But the biggest thing I had to confront was my own aversion to seeing my spit in significant quantity.

Every day, my spit looks different when it's in a cup. It can be kind of icky, but like my body, it's ultimately a work of avant-garde art. It's swirled with food and stained with rainbow hues from liquids such as coffee or soup. I could produce spit that looks like soft dollops of cappuccino foam after talking animatedly with someone, or it could have solid pieces of mucus, or it could form abstract sculptures as the spit soaks up tissues that I stick inside the cup to prevent spillage. This is something that my body produces on the regular, and seeing it outside of my body places it in an entirely different context. Using the spit cup is a creative process.

Being so familiar with my spit every day demonstrates the amazing beauty of the human body. Saliva serves me, and I am also at its mercy. My spit cup is an indicator of my disability's progression. My spit cup is also a public signifier that this bodymind is hella unique.

When we think of interdependence, we often think about relationships with people and with communities. Giving and receiving help from friends, neighbors, and family link us all together. As my body has changed, I have become more dependent on objects and have grown to appreciate them as part of this complex infrastructure that facilitates my survival. My cyborg body is tethered to orbiting satellites. These bits of hardware, machines, and everyday objects may not live and breathe, but they are a part of me. They simultaneously ground me and liberate me. They center me and allow me to make the most out of my life.

> AS MY BODY HAS CHANGED, I HAVE BECOME MORE DEPENDENT ON OBJECTS AND HAVE GROWN TO APPRECIATE THEM AS PART OF THIS COMPLEX INFRASTRUCTURE THAT FACILITATES MY SURVIVAL.

Like breathing, swallowing saliva is an invisible, taken-for-granted task most bodies perform all the time. As I grow weaker, I become more in tune with the constant rhythms of breathing, swallowing, eating, and talking. I appreciate the sophistication of how each single action is interlocked with others and how fragile any person can be. My disability forces me to listen to my body and MacGyver the hell out of it. I am as grateful for my cyborg existence as I am grateful to my spit cup.

How do things like straw bans impact disabled people?

Over the last few years, straw bans have gained popularity as a means of helping to reduce waste that ends up causing irreparable damage to the environment. These bans have meant that many restaurants have either switched from plastic straws to paper straws or elected to ditch straws entirely.

But these types of environmental bans may not fully take people with disabilities into account. Those who have mobility or strength issues, for example, may not be able to hold a cup, making it impossible or very difficult for them to drink without a straw. Single-use plastic straws were, in fact, originally used to help disabled people.

While there are certainly disabled people who can use alternative straws, the single-use, bendable plastic straw allows the greatest accessibility for those who need them. Not only are these individuals able to drink liquids safely this way, but such straws also reduce the risk of injury, allergic reaction, infection, and aspiration—all of which could be fatal. If a disabled person says they need a single-use plastic straw, it's because they have tried alternatives that do not work, or they know using an alternative will be burdensome or harmful.

Instead of blanket policies, individuals who can forgo straws should do so. Plastic single-use straws should be made available in a way that lets everyone make their own decisions about their needs, without having to explain their disability to acquire one.

BODY TALK

FAQS

THE WHITE RABBIT

BY JOHN MCGINTY

I, as a Deaf person, went to London with my family on vacation when I was ten or eleven years old. My grandmother decided to take me to see the musical *The Phantom of the Opera*. The moment I sat down, I realized there was no interpreter, nor were there any captions to help me understand what was happening. But as soon as the curtain went up and the story started to unfold, it was so visual that my original concern vanished.

This was my lightbulb moment. I realized that this was exactly what I wanted to do. I wanted to act, to be part of that world.

I was actually born hearing, and my whole family is hearing. I was quite ill when I was an infant. I took a medication that was supposed to improve my health, and it did, but as a side effect, I lost my hearing.

From pre-K through kindergarten, my parents sent me to a school in Cleveland, Ohio, that used sign language only. American Sign Language (ASL) was the first language I acquired. From first through fourth grade, I went to a school with an oral program that focused more on hearing and speech (a.k.a. listening and speaking). Sign language was not part of its teaching method. During that time, both of my siblings went to a private school, and I wanted to attend it, too, because I wanted to do the same thing as them. However, when I arrived at that school, I had to take fourth grade over again. I was the only Deaf person, and there were no support services: no interpreters, no notetakers, no FM systems (wireless assistive hearing devices that enhance the use of hearing aids). Nothing. Just me alone in a classroom. I stayed for fourth and fifth grade. I fell behind because I could not understand what the teacher was saying, I was not able to interact with my peers, and

I was not involved in the school. I even air-played my clarinet in my music class. My parents noticed.

Things changed in the sixth grade. My parents sent me to a Deaf residential school called Clarke School for the Deaf in Northampton, Massachusetts. Like the school I attended from first through fourth grade, this one focused more on speech and hearing. It was at this school that I rediscovered my passion for acting. As much as theater inspired me at a young age, at first I did not have the self-confidence to get involved. I was involved in a lot of activities at my school, like playing soccer and taking science classes. But even though I had two teachers ask me separately if I was planning to audition for the school play, I laughed and said it was not going to happen. They were doing a production of *Alice in Wonderland*, and I had no confidence at that point. I wondered why someone with incredibly low self-esteem would want to perform in front of a live audience. Who would want to watch me stand on stage with my legs shaking and my teeth chattering?

But those teachers were persistent, and they wore me down. I showed up at auditions and thought mine was probably the worst audition in the history of theater. But I was cast as the White Rabbit. That was the moment my passion for theater was reignited. I realized I could do this.

At that time I considered theater a hobby. It was a fun thing to do, to collaborate with different people, to work on a production. I loved my time on stage in front of the audience, and my self-confidence started to grow. I began to learn who I was and to establish more of an identity. From that time on, I was involved in different school plays and productions.

The Clarke School went up to only the ninth grade, though. That meant that after I graduated, I had to go back to Cleveland to finish high school. I ended up going to a public school, again as the only Deaf person. However, this time, I had an oral interpreter, which is different from a sign language interpreter. An oral interpreter sits and listens to what is said and reproduces it on their lips. This meant I was focused on lip-reading someone for eight hours a day. (A funny story: One time, in an honors chemistry class, my teacher explained how a "bond" works in H_2O. My interpreter misunderstood my teacher and thought he said, "bomb." Can you imagine thinking you would explode by drinking water?)

But even though I had assistance from an oral interpreter in my classes, my high school career was even more challenging than all my previous years in the education system. It was not just that I was the only Deaf person. I had also missed out on socializing at the start of ninth grade, when my class-mates had all started their high school careers. My peers had already made their friends and formed their cliques. Coming in as a tenth grader made finding my place difficult. At the start of my time at the public high school, there were few Deaf people living in Cleveland, at least that I was aware of, so I was not really out there aggressively trying to find people like myself to make a connection with.

And there was another thing I was worried about: At the *Deaf* school, I could get big acting roles, but at a *hearing* high school, would I still have the same opportunities?

It turned out that hearing casting directors and teachers did not really comprehend how much work I had put into being an actor as a Deaf person. And more, I did not do a good job of self-advocating. I just took what was offered. My teachers had never dealt with a Deaf actor before, and I had never worked with someone who had never dealt with a Deaf actor before. I had to start building those bridges. I had to get us all to the other end. I had to teach them about what I needed.

It was difficult for me to ask for what I needed, namely getting an ASL interpreter for equal access to the discussions. I was not confident enough. At high school theater rehearsals, I would feel way behind and completely lost because I did not know where I was supposed to go or what was going on with the whole show. So even though I had previously been able to build up my self-esteem with acting, it was becoming another source of self-doubt and frustration.

As challenging as it was to face this experience over and over again, it led to another lightbulb moment: I realized that anything was possible. That anyone, whether they were Deaf or hearing or had any other abilities, could be involved. This was monumental for me. Up until this point, I had only been in shows with all-Deaf casts. I was grateful to my high school drama teacher for giving me small chances, which would make bigger and better things possible.

And then in my senior year of high school, I was offered a spot in a production of *Robin Hood* with the Cleveland SignStage after seeing a casting notice from them and auditioning. My high school allowed me to go on tour with the show if I kept up with my coursework remotely. I did not set foot in school for an entire semester, but I was still able to graduate on time.

That was an amazing time in my life, and it was the experience I needed in order to realize that I could be a professional actor. I also knew I needed to be practical and have a backup plan. So I went to college and majored in finance. Just in case theater did not work out. Before college, Deaf culture was not something I self-identified with. I was a Deaf person, but I was not *culturally* Deaf until college. Up to that point I was still on a journey, trying to figure out who I was in the education system and what language suited me. When I arrived at Northeastern University, my identity as a Deaf person was very clear, in part because there was a greater population of Deaf people who used sign language. But even though I had learned sign language at my first school, I had stopped signing because my environments had shifted to focus instead on speech and hearing. At first, it was tough for me to communicate with my Deaf peers who used American Sign Language as their primary language. It was quite remarkable how welcome and patient people were while I was picking it back up. That was when I realized ASL was the language that best suited me. I had come full circle.

My first big acting break came during my junior year of college, when I got a role in a Deaf West musical production of *Pippin* in Los Angeles. Since then, my work on- and offstage has been about collaboration and continuing education. I was a late bloomer as a Deaf person, but I figured out who I was along the way. And I continue to use my experiences in my theater career to support the Deaf community, to meet a wide array of people, and to work toward becoming a better person within the Deaf community.

After the Deaf West production of *Pippin*, I saw a call for auditions for an upcoming production of *The Hunchback of Notre Dame* in California. The director was someone I had met in a workshop, and I thought, *You know what? I can do this show.* I went ahead and emailed the director, asking, "Have you ever thought about having a Deaf actor play that role?" After all, the main character, Quasimodo, in Victor Hugo's original work is Deaf, though he is not often portrayed that way. I threw a bunch of ideas out there to show how it could work. Being solution oriented is important—if you see a problem, offer solutions. You can really open people's minds.

The director responded, "Well, come audition. Why not? Let's see."

I went in. I got a callback. I got the role.

I was the first Deaf actor to play Quasimodo in a musical. Since then, two or three other Deaf people have played that role in regional productions. That is a huge win, and I am proud that my work helped pave the way for other Deaf actors to pursue the roles they want.

In my Broadway debut, a revival of *Children of a Lesser God*, I struggled to find a way to speak up and be an advocate. I played Orin Dennis, who is a loud and proud Deaf advocate, but me? I was the opposite. The role of Orin pushed me to better understand the importance of speaking up, following my instincts, and not worrying about other people's hurt feelings when pushing to do what is right. Sometimes it is necessary to step on a toe in order to break down barriers and overcome obstacles. And the next year, I joined another Broadway revival, *King Lear*.

I have also become deeply involved in the Actors' Equity Association, because I wanted to improve and expand the world of diversity and inclusion. I am the first and only Deaf person to win a seat on the council. There is so much opportunity to be had for Deaf actors, and I am looking forward to continuing to find places where I can offer collaborative solutions to make roles more accessible and available. I am also eager to continue breaking down the unnecessary barriers between the hearing world and the Deaf world, including educating casting directors about the costs associated with accessibility. It is an additional burden to bring in interpreters. But I offer understanding, coupled with a new perspective: "If you decide that you want to put on a musical, you hire a pianist for rehearsals. How is this any different? What is the difference between an interpreter and a pianist?" See a problem, offer a solution.

I am really excited about this next generation of people who are doing inclusive and diverse theater. I am trying to be a pioneer for them too, because we cannot sit back and wait. We have to do something now.

For those who are Deaf or who have other abilities, here's some advice: just find joy. Find what it is that you love, whether that is acting, writing, directing, producing, whatever, and get involved. When you decide that you are going to audition for something, be yourself and make the role your own.

Do not wait. Life is going to pass you by, so just do the things you love. It is easy to talk about things rather than do them, but if you take the plunge and go for it, things are going to work out. It may not be how you originally envisioned it, but things will fall into place.

Collaboration is important. If you are offering ideas and your peers do not quite follow your train of thought, just keep your mind and your heart open. You will find yourself in a better position to work on other projects in the future.

And last but not least, it is important to own yourself. You can make the world a better place if you just show people who you are. And they need you to do that. We are listening to your story. Find your voice in whatever language fits you. Make them listen.

If you need help, I am here and waiting for you.

ROARS AND WHISPERS BY KELLY BASTOW

FIVE ASS-ENTIAL TYRA TIPS FOR BETTER BODY IMAGE

BY TYRA BANKS

1. Make a list of what you love about your body. Add something new every month.

Sit down and take the time to do this. Get a pen and paper, and set a timer for five minutes. Write down as many things as you can think of that you like about yourself, and it is OK if it is just one, then post that list someplace you'll see it every day (like on the bathroom mirror). Once a month, revisit the list and add something new.

2. Self-care, boo!

Get your nails did, get your hair did, take a bubble bath, take a long nap, eat a cupcake, binge a season of *Big Little Lies* (or *Top Model*, just sayin'), read an entire book in one sitting, spend some time alone. Whatever it is that makes you feel good and rested, carve out the time to do it.

3. Fake it till you make it.

Pretend you're confident and love your body. Next time you're at the pool, stroll around without a cover-up instead of hiding behind a towel. Do all the things you think a body-confident woman would do, and you might start believing yourself.

4. Stop talking ish about other women.

If you find yourself wanting to criticize the way someone else looks, just stop. Change the subject. Or even better, say something nice.

5. Ditch the triggers.

Try to cut out the things and people that make you feel bad. If you have a 105-pound friend who's always talking about how she could lose a few, take a break. Maybe she's not your best going-out-to-dinner buddy. If Instagram makes you feel sad, stop the scroll.

This piece was previously published in Perfect Is Boring *by Tyra Banks and Carolyn London.*

LOOKING "STRAIGHT"

BY JOURDAIN SEARLES

I've always hated the way I look in pictures. With optic nerve atrophy, blindness, and nystagmus in one eye and nearsightedness in the other, getting my eyes to point in the same direction for photographs has always been a struggle.

Before smartphones, I would take all my photographs with a tiny purple Kodak camera. When taking my own picture, I enjoyed orchestrating the composition of my own image. I could never trust the photographers on picture day, and the feeling was mutual. They would beg me to make my eyes "straight," and I never knew how to tell them that it was impossible to do that unless I was taking the photo myself. I created tricks to force my eyes to look one way, straining them in the process, all in the effort to appear normal.

When early social media platform Myspace was created, I would take pictures over and over again, not stopping until I looked some semblance of "normal" as I understood it. Now taking a hundred selfies until you find the right angle is common, and I can't help but feel like a trendsetter. It's a bitter victory, but I'll take it.

Normal was never something I could attain, but I yearned for it. Relatives and friends alike would call me "cockeyed" and make jokes that were meant to be playful. I would never fake a laugh, but I would smile, hiding my anger behind my teeth. I had to develop a thick, rubbery skin—nothing could get through, and everything bounced off into the distance. I hated my eyes, my body, but I forced myself to wear an armor of confidence. I had to. I wasn't just a disabled girl; I was a black girl, a fat girl, a girl with short kinky hair that looked lifeless with a relaxer. I had big feet, a wide nose, and a wide heart-shaped face.

For the longest time, I thought my appearance was some kind of cosmic joke, a punishing imperfection that could be remedied only by perfect grades and a denial of all pleasures. I became an angry overachiever, always sensitive, always feeling judged about what my eyes could and couldn't do.

I do wonder what it would be like if we just let ourselves look as weird as we feel. We don't look perfect—none of us do. So why do pictures have to be? A picture can't convey how adorable I often am. I'm short with a loud voice and a brightness that not even the best photographer can capture, even when my eyes are "straight."

The upside to being half-blind is that no one knows you are at first glance. The downside to being half-blind is . . . no one knows you are at first glance. It was a constant point of conflict. I wanted to be normal. I also wanted to be noticed—but only for my best qualities. I never wanted to be noticed in the "bad" way. I never wanted to see that look of pity on anyone's face. Or worse, confused anger when my eyes didn't move the way someone thought they should.

But regardless of what I wanted, it kept happening anyway. During school assemblies, plays, and movie screenings, teachers would walk me to the front. I sat in the front row in every class. My classmates were often angry at me for what they perceived as special treatment. Meanwhile, I saw it as an embarrassing burden that stopped boys from liking me. It felt like everyone hated me for my apparent deception. They didn't believe I was blind. I didn't have a cane. I didn't read in braille. I wrote stories all the time—surely I could see the words I was writing! I could feel them wondering, *So what's the problem?*

Being a black girl exacerbated everything. We are already thought of as vessels of attitude and anger. We are treated as if our pain doesn't matter or that we have the supernatural ability to withstand pain more easily than others do. Our bodies are always a topic of conversation, our curves treated as dangerous. I wasn't just a disabled girl. I was a disabled curvy black girl—the kind often stereotyped with finger snapping and neck rolling, especially in the primarily white environments where I lived. And I had no road map to addressing my intersections. Instead of feeling whole, I saw my identities as separate, and I struggled with the contradiction of needing help while being seen as someone who could take care of herself. It was difficult, feeling so judged and vulnerable. To deal with it, I turned to writing. I would imagine myself as a girl with a support system, friends who saw how complicated I was and loved me for it. Writing can be a safe haven that way. It doesn't matter if you're good with words or not. Self-expression doesn't have to be perfect.

In primary school, I was assigned a disability specialist by the public school system. My family never had much money, but part of the reason my mother insisted we live in our particular zip code was so I could access the best counseling and low-vision devices for my eyesight at no cost to us. I had three vision specialists throughout my time in primary school, and I loved all of them. They were, in a sense, my first therapists. I told them about my fears, dreams, and confusions. Their kindness and patience kept me going.

I was born with my disability, so my mother always blamed herself for my low vision. She had a lot of trouble communicating her emotions to me effectively, so I didn't understand her feelings about my eyes until I was much older. She would mainly lash out with physical and emotional abuse and make amends later. She wouldn't apologize, exactly—my mother expressed her love through sales and intense clearance-rack browsing. After days when things had been particularly tense with us, she would arrive home late, carting big bags full of clothes from Citi Trends or Marshalls. She always lived by the mentality that life was miserable anyway, so she might as well do what she wanted—even if it meant being a working-class shopaholic. She never asked me what sort of clothes I was into, so I often ended up dressing like a mini version of her.

I liked the clothes at first. They made me feel shiny and important. I gained a sense of confidence from their loudness. I loved pink, orange, and bright red. I loved the barrettes and the sparkles. Dressing this way made me feel like I didn't have to shrink myself for being different. But eventually I realized my mom's way of dressing wasn't for me. She liked traditionally feminine clothes: bedazzled jeans, pink tracksuits, flowery tops, and eccentric wedges. She liked glittery lip gloss and flashy impractical purses with sharp gold zippers that cut my hand and pockets that weren't big enough for my books. The clothes flattered my body but not my spirit.

At the time, I was getting into rock music—Pixies, Modest Mouse, Hole. The angst in the music matched my own. I could cry to the music or wail. I was also getting into women. I would develop crushes on my female friends and had no clue what to do about it. I realized that I was bisexual at the same time that I realized I loved rock music, but my clothes didn't reflect my desires or my interests. I was a queer punk riot grrrl in the clothes of a high femme straight girl. But why make myself more different than I already was? Pressing myself into a straight femme box was a way of closeting myself. I would try to counter my internal desires by presenting as a very straitlaced "normal girl" on the outside.

My real self kept spilling out, though, mainly in the stories I wrote. I wrote about teen lovers, rock stars, strippers, and rebellious artists. I wrote about sex and passion and anger. I wrote wild things that I would rarely show to anyone except a few close friends and the like-minded moody teens in my message board community. We talked about the kind of lives we'd like to lead when we were older. I also got close to my younger brother—he would share records with me and introduce me to even more bands. He stopped letting our mom dress him before I did, and I ended up following his lead. It was around that time that I began my '90s-rock T-shirt collection. Later, when I was in college, he taught me how to stretch my earlobes and encouraged me to get facial piercings. I didn't take him up on that until much later. I have a medusa piercing right in the middle of my face. I love it.

Still, there are times when I wonder if my rock style is a new kind of shield—a way to make myself feel less vulnerable. When I wear dresses and heels for important events, that is when I feel most exposed. For me, it's easy to feel comfortable in a giant PJ Harvey T-shirt and much scarier to put on a sparkly dress. A body-con dress says, "I want to be seen!" Sometimes I worry what parts of myself become exposed with that vulnerability. There's a lot of internal drama that comes with being noticed.

One morning in high school, when my vision teacher suggested I buy a cane as a marker so that strangers would know that I was blind, I flatly declined. I wanted to look as normal as possible. I wore designer bifocals, as if the fashion logo would distract everyone from the fact that I had four lenses instead of two. (When people called me "four-eyes," I would laugh—they weren't looking hard enough.)

Now, in my late twenties, I'm invisible the way I always wanted to be. No one seems to know how bad my vision is, no matter how much I talk about it. Acquaintances whisper about me having an attitude for not speaking to them (forgetting the fact that I probably couldn't see them). When I'm walking and looking at my phone, strangers get angry at me, not knowing that I'm using the navigation to guide me—not browsing the web. In a way, my caneless existence has worked too well.

At this point, I realize that whether I buy a cane or not is irrelevant. I can't change the way people see me. The only thing that I can do is embrace being comfortable with myself. It's easier said than done. I know the ache of wanting others to like you and the pain that comes with rejection. But I also know that many of the people who rejected me then look up to me now. Another bitter victory. I was a poor blind kid, and I made it all the way to New York City with the help of friends and family who understand me. I can't control the people who are always going to have a bad reaction to my eyes. All I can control is how I move in the world.

These days, I dress for myself. With my piercings, shaved head, fishnet stockings, and band T-shirts, I feel like the real me. Sometimes I even post photos that show my eyes looking in different directions. I know I can't like myself all the time, but sometimes is enough for me.

HOW ANYONE CAN HELP TRANS PEOPLE IN THEIR LIVES, WRITTEN FROM THE PERSPECTIVE OF A TRANS MAN

BY GAVIN GRIMM

- **Believe them.**

If a trans person tells you what their truth is, it is not up for debate, interpretation, or analysis. It is a statement of fact, and trans people are not required to prove, explain, or quantify their identities or expressions. There is, after all, no wrong way to be trans.

Additionally, even if it seems sudden to you or isn't obvious based on your perception of gender—which was influenced by a binary, trans-exclusionary society—I promise that a trans person has a much better handle on their feelings and identity than anyone could possibly have from an external point of view. Believe them.

- **Make an effort with your language.**

Make sure you are making a conscious effort to use the correct name, pronouns, and language with any trans person in your life. Is a trans man standing beside three women? Then *ladies* is not an appropriate grouping term. Has a trans person told you that words like *dude* or *bro* feel uncomfortably masculine? Then stop using it for their sake, and don't argue that they're wrong. Apologize, modify your language, and move on.

- **Ask them what they need.**

Ask your trans friend, coworker, child, whoever it is, what it is you can do to support them. Many times, trans people will be clear about the language they prefer, but not always. When in doubt, it's best to never assume. You risk embarrassing or even endangering that person. Sometimes people are out in some circles, but not in others.

- **Be careful with their information.**

If you know someone who is trans, then you may also know other private details about them. This might include the name they were given at birth (also called a "dead name") if they decided to change their name (and not every trans person does), or you may have or know about photos of the person before their transition. Remember that this information is private and personal and can cause harm if it is spread around. Do not disclose someone's private information, including their trans status, to anyone else. It is not OK, and it is not your place, unless you have clear and explicit permission from the trans person.

- **Do not ask inappropriate questions.**

Because I am a trans person, confused non-trans (or cis) people often ask me invasive, inappropriate, or otherwise unnecessary questions about trans bodies and lives. Don't be that person. It is inappropriate to ask trans people what medical steps they have or have not taken to transition. It is personal information. It is inappropriate to ask trans people what is in their pants. It is personal information. It is inappropriate to ask trans people things like what their dead name was. It is *all* personal information. If a trans person wants to share any of these details, they will do so when they feel safe. Some trans people don't share these kinds of things, and some trans people do. Ultimately you are not entitled to know any of it.

- **Do not burden the trans people in your life with your quest for education.** In our society, it is up to every individual to learn about the people we may encounter as we move through our beautiful world. This includes trans people. It is a duty for each of us to have at least a basic education in gender diversity. It can seem tempting to go to the nearest trans person and ask them all your burning questions, but trans people are often already unfairly burdened every day with explaining themselves to cis people. So take it upon yourself to learn, but use resources intended for that education, not your trans coworker. There are endless supplies of resources made by trans people for cis people that can be found for free on the internet and can answer many questions you may have.

  Additionally, there are trans people doing this educational work at conferences, events, schools, workplaces, and so on. These people may do this education for free, though often it's a means of income. If you are a cis person, it is a wonderful show of allyship to pay a trans person for the education they are providing for you. Paid lessons or seminars by trans people not only are informative but also financially support a community that is historically low income or financially insecure due to transphobia making jobs harder to find and harder to do for trans people.

- **Do not burden trans people with depictions of community violence.** You're on Facebook. You see a news story. "Trans Person Murdered." You might think that it's horrible and that you should send it to [trans friend] right away because [trans friend] is trans, and wouldn't they like to hear the news?

  Don't. Not every trans person is plugged in 24/7 to the latest community news, but many are. And those who aren't often abstain for personal reasons, like mental health. Those who are already know. Even if they haven't heard about this specific instance, they know they are at an exponentially higher risk for violence than their cis peers. There is no need to point out additional trauma in the trans community if you are not a trans person. You can of course share such posts, share your own personal thoughts on your own personal Facebook page, but do not burden the trans people in your life with this trauma. It is not the job of cis people to remind trans people that our lives are in danger.

- **Do not bring trans people into situations that can be dangerous for them.** Is there a family gathering where conservative members of the family will be present? Don't force a trans kid to make nice with people who openly and regularly decry the community. If a trans kid says they aren't comfortable around certain people, respect their wishes. It's not about not wanting to be with family or not wanting to be social; it's about safety and self-preservation.

Are you hanging out with your trans friend and considering inviting another friend, who happens to be notoriously transphobic, to join you? Don't! The safety of the trans person in your life is infinitely more important than your desire to hang out with your transphobic friend.

- **Do not police a trans person's expression.** What society deems as "for men" or "for women" is, at best, a marketing scheme. It's not an evolutionary construct for men to like Axe body spray and cropped hair and for women to like flowers and dresses. Just like cis men and cis women, trans people are allowed to express their gender identities in whatever way they want, period. Trans men are allowed to have interests or expressions that society considers feminine. Trans women are allowed to have interests or expressions that society considers masculine. And nonbinary people are allowed to like whatever they like and express themselves however they want without casting an alliance to the binary of boy or girl.

Again, just believe trans people. Believe we know how we want to present ourselves to the world and are capable of doing that, because we do and we are. Don't warn a trans boy that if he wears a really cute pair of earrings, he is going to get misgendered. He knows that. He doesn't care; he likes those earrings, and being misgendered doesn't mean he isn't a boy.

BELIEVE TRANS PEOPLE.

- **Do not apply a pressure to "pass" to any trans person.**

Passing is the concept of being visually read as the gender with which you identify. This concept is one that means survival for many trans people, but it is also a concept composed almost entirely of a binary, cis-centric stereotype in society. For that reason, many trans people do not want to, or cannot, fit into the narrow box society determines is an acceptable man or woman. This means that trans people who are gender nonconforming, nonbinary, or are limited in their transitional options or desires may often fall outside of these categories visually.

A trans man might prefer not to, or be unable to, bind his chest. A trans woman might prefer not to, or be unable to, shave her face. A nonbinary person might appear outwardly and from a stereotypical perspective to be more masculine or feminine aligned, but may prefer gender-neutral pronouns and language, or language different from what people may expect.

A trans person, above all, is never required to meet a cis-dictated gold standard of femininity or masculinity or neutrality to be considered valid.

- **Let the trans people in your life lead the way.**

Just like cis people, trans people know themselves. And just like cis people, a trans person's identity and personal perception or presentation might evolve over the course of their journey. There is nothing wrong with that, as there are so few permanent states of being. Let trans people explore themselves and their identities, whether they are static from day one or they try out many different labels as they find what fits. Allow the trans people in your life to tell you what language honors them and how best to support them. Raise your voice as a cis person when you see transphobia occurring. Learn how to spot it.

Believe trans people and follow their lead. Being trans is joyful. It can be scary, and it can be hard. But above all, it is beautiful, and seldom the most interesting thing about a person.

MY BACK-BRACE YEAR: HOW I LEARNED TO STAND TALL, EVEN WHILE HUNCHED

BY KATE BIGAM KAPUT

The room is silent aside from regular classroom sounds: pencils scribbling furiously against lined notebook paper, backpacks zipping and unzipping as their owners rummage through them, the occasional sniffle or sneeze from a fellow student.

Our homeroom, led by the strict and humorless sixth-grade science teacher Mr. Reilly, is made up of all the students at the start of the alphabet—last names Adama through Cravitz—and I am right in the middle, Bigam. Our classmates with last names *D* to *Z* are luckier than we are; they're allowed to talk in their homerooms, or they watch movies or play games. Per Mr. Reilly's rules, though, we're not allowed to do anything in our homeroom except work or read. *Silently.*

Our homeroom is almost entirely quiet—except for me.

I can't help that my plastic back brace sometimes squeaks when I breathe—seemingly at random times. *Creaaaaaaak* in, *creaaaaaaak* out, over and over and over. I try to hold my breath. I try to breathe more slowly, more quietly. I try to steady my brace and muffle the squeaks by putting my hands on the hard, warm plastic. I try everything I can think of, but still, I squeak. And I think Mr. Reilly assumes I'm doing it on purpose.

Because when I start to squeak, my classmates start to giggle. Sometimes they giggle before the squeaking even begins, wondering if it'll happen today. In a homeroom as boring as ours, the weird, shrill noises coming from my torso are, to my humiliation, one of the only exciting things to happen in the forty-five minutes spent in Mr. Reilly's homeroom each day. They give my classmates something to pay attention to, something to laugh at—and they give me something to stress about. *Will today be one of the days I squeak?*

There's a small storage room attached to our homeroom, and sometimes, when he's feeling nice, Mr. Reilly lets me go in there and take off my brace. I rip open the loud Velcro fasteners that keep it closed tight around my hips and back, then I slide it out from under my T-shirt and leave it in the storage room until the bell rings, when I slip back into the brace before heading outside to catch the bus home. These days are such a relief: no squeaking, no sweating under the plastic, no physical difference between me and anyone else.

Most of the time, though, when I ask if I can take off my brace, Mr. Reilly says no. He's not being mean, not really; he just knows the rules, and if there's one thing Mr. Reilly loves, it's rules. He knows as well as I do that I'm supposed to wear the brace for twenty-three hours a day, removing it only to shower. The more I wear it, the more likely it is to help straighten my crooked spine as I grow. That's the hope, anyway.

Some days, inexplicably, Mr. Reilly says no, sending me into the storage room to work by myself so my squeaks won't disrupt the class. Outwardly, I try to take it in stride, but nothing feels more alienating than being separated from my classmates so that I can squeak in silence, stewing over the way this stupid back brace is ruining my life.

I am eleven years old, and I got the brace two months before I started sixth grade. I went to the doctor's office to see whether I had my usual bout of seasonal bronchitis—and I did, but that was more easily treatable than the *other* condition that my X-ray revealed. My pediatrician diagnosed me with severe adolescent idiopathic scoliosis, otherwise known as a curvature of the spine, and sent me to an orthopedic specialist the very next week. By the end of the month, I was being fitted for a back brace.

It all happened so quickly that there wasn't even time for me to feel horrified or embarrassed or afraid. It was kind of like reading a book about someone else's life, in which the plot points move forward, the story progresses quickly, and it all wraps up with a neat, tidy ending: me, in a back brace.

Except the story isn't over—not even close. I still have all of sixth grade left to go. This is my life now, even though I have barely had any time to process the fact that it's real.

My mom and my doctors explain it to me like this: instead of growing nice and straight like most kids' spines, mine is growing in the shape of an *S*, pushing my right shoulder up and my left hip out.

It isn't visibly obvious, and it doesn't hurt yet—which is why I didn't know I had it—but my new orthopedist says that as I continue to grow, my spine will continue to twist and it will, indeed, start to cause me pain. He also says that if left untreated, my scoliosis will result in severe deformation, so he hopes that bracing my back for twenty-three hours a day will straighten my spine as it grows and prevent the need for corrective surgery down the road.

The day of my diagnosis, those words—*severe deformation*—ring loudly in my brain as I try to convince myself that wearing a back brace for a few years will be way better than a lifetime of whatever might happen to me if I don't. As much as I hate the idea of starting school with a brace, I hate the idea of back surgery even more—so I agree to it, begrudgingly, like I have any choice in the matter to begin with.

Before I get fitted for the brace, my mom makes me read *Deenie*, Judy Blume's young adult book about a girl who gets a back brace in middle school. I'm sure my mom didn't read this book before she gave it to me, or else she wouldn't have given it to me at all: Deenie's back brace is huge and metal. There's headgear involved.

As I read the book, I am *absolutely horrified*, even though my doctor has assured me that my brace will be made of plastic. My mom, frantic and contrite, apologizes a dozen times, insisting that she thought I would benefit from Deenie's story even if the details of our braces aren't the same. All I can think is *Thank goodness for evolving technology, or this brace could be even worse.* It's a small comfort, at least.

But the day I am fitted for my brace is one of the worst days of my young life. I lie down on a cold metal table, wearing only my underwear and an undershirt, while medical staff wrap me in thick, wet strips of goopy fabric that will harden to form the mold they'll use to create my back brace, fitted specially to my body.

The process reminds me of the papier-mâché projects I've done in art class; I feel like a human piñata. As the goopy fabric hardens around me, I start to feel hot, uncomfortable, and claustrophobic. I start to sweat and then to cry. Is this over yet? Is this what wearing my brace is going to feel like?

When they're done, they saw open the side of the papier-mâché mold, releasing me from its clutches and holding up a perfect replica of my torso. I am free, for now—but not for long.

A week later, my brace is ready for me.

Starting middle school was already scary enough, because in my hometown, two local elementary schools combine into one for the start of sixth grade. That means a whole new crop of classmates—and now they'll only know me as the girl with a back brace.

I've never been popular, but I've never been totally *un*popular, either. I'm right in the middle, generally well liked but never invited to parties; mostly, I'm kind of shy and awkward. When I don't know what to say to people, I just blush and laugh, like a big dork. Still, new classmates meant new opportunities for first impressions, so I hoped middle school would be a turning point for me. I spent all summer imagining how I'd reinvent myself when the school year began.

Now, though, I'm doomed, and it's all because of this back brace. How am I ever going to become popular if I'm wearing the equivalent of a full-body cast beneath my clothes every day? I'll probably become a total social pariah.

Unlike Deenie's brace, my brace will be worn under my clothes, so it's supposed to be hidden. "Other people won't even be able to tell!" my doctor promises me, but he's not a sixth-grade girl. *Everyone* can tell.

When I sit down in classes, the top of the brace separates itself a bit from my skin, creating a small tent beneath my shirt that makes me look like I'm wearing a cardboard box as a backpack. I try to sit up straighter to minimize the effect, but I can't really sit up straight; that's why I have a back brace to begin with.

There are little breathing holes peppered throughout the brace, dime-sized spots in the plastic to keep me from suffocating in this thing. My friends have figured out where the holes are, though, so sometimes, in the middle of class, someone pokes a pencil into my side. Luckily, no potential bullies have figured out this trick—but my friends think it's hilarious.

When I change into my gym clothes in the locker room (I can't *believe* that wearing this thing hasn't even gotten me out of gym), my female class-mates can see my brace in all its plasticky glory, like I'm some kind of weird robot.

And, of course, there's the squeaking in homeroom, so that even if you can't *see* my back brace, you can occasionally *hear* it.

Just this year, Disney released the animated musical *The Hunchback of Notre Dame*, starring the hunchback of Notre Dame himself, Quasimodo. Even though Quasimodo turns out to be the hero of the story, I don't want to be compared to him—but I *am* a hunchback, as my cousins like to point out. They have taken to calling me Quasi, and I pray it's a nickname no one at my school will ever think of.

Slowly, though, wearing the brace becomes my new normal. I still hate it: it sticks to me when I sweat, and it chafes against me, and the thin skin around my rib cage often gets caught in the biggest of the breathing holes; I always have ugly purplish bruises there now.

But mostly, I've gotten used to the brace's existence, and my classmates have, too. It's more like a prop than a conversation piece. No one really talks about it anymore; it's just *there*.

I'm caught off guard when one day halfway through the school year, a kid named Mario asks me, point-blank, "What happens when you take your brace off? Do you even have a spine?" Mario is really cute, and he has a lot of popular friends; his question isn't mean-spirited, but I know if he had asked me at the beginning of the year, I would've been mortified. I would've done my signature blush and giggle, not knowing how to respond.

Now, though, I just laugh.

"Mario," I tell him, speaking slowly and looking him in the eyes. "If I didn't have a spine, I wouldn't be standing up. I'd be, like, a puddle of a person on the floor. When I take off my back brace, I look exactly the same as I look right now—just without a back brace."

He looks confused; he looks embarrassed. Some of our classmates hear the conversation and start to laugh, and even though I feel a little bad for making him look dumb, I'm proud of myself, too. I responded confidently and with a little bit of humor—and it wasn't weird or awkward. It just *was*.

A week later, in art class, I tell my friend Mariah about the nickname my cousins have given me: Quasi, short for Quasimodo, like the hunchback of Notre Dame. I don't know why I decide to tell her this; it just sort of pops out. Mariah is more popular than I am, but she's nice, too, so when she starts to laugh—hilarious, riotous, raucous laughter—I start to panic.

And then I realize she's not laughing *at* me, she's just *laughing*. Because it's *funny*.

I start laughing with her, and suddenly I don't hate the nickname so much anymore. Soon I stop worrying that someone from school might start to call me that—but no one ever does.

There's no way around it: wearing a back brace kind of sucks. But you know what actually doesn't suck as much as I thought it would? Being the kid at school who wears a back brace.

> YOU KNOW WHAT ACTUALLY DOESN'T SUCK AS MUCH AS I THOUGHT IT WOULD? BEING THE KID AT SCHOOL WHO WEARS A BACK BRACE.

Sixth grade is more than halfway over before I realize, with surprise, no one makes fun of me for it. No one really pays it much attention at all, and when they do, it's pretty good-natured.

When I am older—when I am twenty or thirty, ages I can barely imagine myself being since I'm eleven—I will still think back on this time in my life and wonder how I got so lucky. Why wasn't I bullied? Why didn't anyone tease me? How did I make it through middle school unscathed when *I wore a giant plastic back brace every day?* It seems almost unfathomable.

Middle schoolers can be brutal. Why haven't they been so to me?

My first explanation—and I'm pretty sure it's accurate—has to do with the family who lives across the street from me. They have four sons and one daughter, all of them good-looking and athletic and popular, and one of them, Johnny, is in my grade. He's a jock, and we're not really friends, but we've known each other since we were babies. I know he would never be openly mean to me, and I bet he wouldn't let his friends make fun of me, either.

That's the first reason, I think—but even at age eleven, I can recognize that the other reason no one makes fun of me has to do with *me*.

I used to be quiet and meek, shy and awkward. But somehow, throughout the course of the year, I have gotten stronger. I'm not scared anymore. At the start of sixth grade, I was so worried about life with a back brace that I set myself up for all the worst-case scenarios: the teasing, the squeaking, the bruising, the poking, even the asking of truly absurd questions like "Do you have a spine?"

But you know what? A lot of those things happened—and I got through all of them OK.

Somehow, I even found it within me to laugh most of them off—and at some point, I didn't even have to try anymore. Now laughing it off is just my go-to response, and who wants to make fun of someone who doesn't even mind being made fun of? As it turns out, no one.

So, yes, my brace is a bit of a joke—but now it's a joke that's funny to me, too. It makes for a great percussion instrument when we're trying to keep the beat in choir, and balls literally bounce right off me in dodgeball. The squeaking in homeroom is a guaranteed laugh on boring days, and eventually, to everyone else's jealousy, I *do* get out of having to take gym.

In seventh grade, my orthopedist will tell me that the brace isn't working, and I need to undergo major spinal surgery to correct my scoliosis. I won't miss wearing the brace—but I still cry the day my mom tries to throw it away, long after I have healed. Wearing that brace taught me more about myself than I ever could have imagined, and I'm surprised to find that saying goodbye to it almost feels like losing a friend.

Somehow, when I wasn't looking, the tough outer shell I wore around my body translated into a tough outer shell around my personality, too.

I became stronger. I gained a better sense of humor. I found my confidence, which is something most people don't find at age eleven, if ever. And while I never became popular, I did learn how to stand up straight and tall, both figuratively *and* literally—and I have my year in a back brace to thank for all of it.

TWO TOOLS FOR POWERFUL RELAXATION

BY KELLY JENSEN

In stressful situations, our bodies operate in fight, flight, or freeze mode, assessing what's happening and determining whether it's safe or dangerous for us. This instinct comes from the sympathetic nervous system and has been part of our makeup for as long as humans have been around. But sometimes it can overtake our brains, as well as our bodies, leading to unnecessary stress, anxiety, and physical discomfort.

Fortunately, through the parasympathetic nervous system, our bodies have another response mode, called "rest and digest." Learning how to tap into and cultivate this mode is one of the many ways to practice self-care, to de-stress, to reduce anxiety, and to reconnect with your body and mind.

Here are two techniques to try.

1. Alternate Nostril Breathing

Our breath is our power. It helps keep us alive. Often, when we're stressed, our breath grows choppy or inconsistent, but we can play with our breathing to ease our minds and bodies into rest-and-digest mode.

Find a comfortable position—seated, lying down, kneeling, or any other position that allows you to drop your shoulders and find a tall spine. Bring one of your hands to your nose and take three deep inhales and exhales. When you take your fourth inhale, close off your right nostril and exhale from your left nostril. Then inhale through the left nostril, close it off with your fingers, then exhale through the right nostril. Inhale through the right nostril, close it off, and then exhale through the left. You might choose to close your eyes as you continue this pattern of breathing for up to three minutes.

This type of breathing helps ground us in our bodies, since we have to really focus on our breath. That focus helps us tap into the parasympathetic nervous system.

2. Get Upside Down

No, you don't need to do handstands or headstands. Any way you can get your legs above your head will bring the benefits of reverse blood and oxygen flow. This reversal taps into the rest-and-digest mode.

For those without physical limitations, one of the safest and easiest ways to do this is to use a wall. Sit on the floor with one hip pressed flush to a wall and your legs straight out—the leg whose hip is against the wall will also be against the wall. Bend your knees, then allow your elbows to support you as you lower your back to the floor and bring both legs up the wall. Your torso will be perpendicular to the wall, and your legs will be against it. Stay here as long as you'd like, keeping your arms anywhere that feels comfortable. If this doesn't feel great on your back, you can slide a blanket or a pillow under your sacrum or beneath your head. Another option is to drape your legs over the seat of a chair, with your back on the floor.

Electric-wheelchair users can do something similar by elevating their legs above their heart. Those with physical limitations who can comfortably recline may receive the same benefits by putting their hips up on pillows or by draping their legs over either the back or the arms of a couch. Keeping your legs straight isn't the goal; elevating your legs above your heart is, so find the right support and make adjustments that best suit your body.

MY PERREO DE SHAME PLAYLIST

BY LILLIAM RIVERA

Because I'm feeling cute, I enter Forever 21 in search of cheap sunglasses to complete my look. I skim the rack of clothes, not really out to spend much money but feeling good that I can if I want to. Then *the* song plays on the speakers, the one I memorized the lyrics to. You know the one. That song. This song reminds me of the *me* I used to be back in the day. It transports me to a specific time and place. I start to feel a bit unsettled, unmoored, as if the lyrics are changing the chemical components inside me. I locate a mirror to try to find the remnants of the girl I used to be, the girl who spent her high school years avoiding mirrors at all costs, the shy flaca who hid behind baggy clothes and hair that covered most of her face. How did I go from feeling invisible to being the person I'm staring at right now?

I hum the melody of the song and bounce my head to the beat. Music can be a type of time travel. Soon I'm thinking of other songs that conjure up a visceral remix of reggaeton and humiliation. But they aren't all tunes full of sad memories. No. They also recall powerful revelations of sexuality and fierceness.

It's time to take back the playlist and set the story straight, to reveal how I came to love my Boricua body. Go ahead—turn the volume on high.

Ella Le Gusta la Gasolina

I am ten years old, sitting in the living room. The plastic cover on the couch sticks to my thighs. The rotating fan only circulates hot air. I drink my SunnyD, hoping the aspirin-tasting drink will quench my thirst. (It doesn't.) The television is tuned to *El Show de Iris Chacón*. Iris Chacón is known as La Bomba de Puerto Rico and has bodacious curves. She moves her hips so fast, making everything jiggle and rotate in a mesmerizing rhythm. I love Iris because I think she's funny when she performs in her skits. My father loves her for being a bomba. I look down at my nonexistent breasts and curves. I glance at Mami, who is a Latina Audrey Hepburn, petite and slender.

Papi claps after Iris finishes her dance number. "You want to be like her when you grow up?" he asks. "No, you are going to be a good girl."

He's laughing at me and I join him, although I'm not sure what we are actually laughing about. I want to be like Iris Chacón, but Papi thinks she's bad, so I stop.

Listen to El General y Muévelo

I'm thirteen and it's a Saturday. I don't have to get up early, so I stay in bed until my stomach growls. My brothers are already awake. They are watching cartoons and eating cornflakes. I do the same because it's a Saturday and the agenda is there is no agenda. I fix myself a bowl and join my two brothers.

Mami enters with a laundry basket full of clothes. "Go put something on," she says to me. Only to me.

I glance over to my brothers, who are only a couple of years younger. My brothers both wear the exact same thing: a tank top with pajama shorts. I am wearing a long, oversized T-shirt that reaches my knees.

"I told you to go change into your clothes," Mami says.

"Why? Why do I have to change?" I ask.

And Mami gets annoyed with me and snaps back, "Go put on some pants."

My brothers laugh because they don't have to do a damn thing but I have to cover myself, and I don't understand how my legs can be such a problem in my own home. From then on my clothes start to expand. Extra-large T-shirts.

Baggy pants. Hoodies. My body has developed, and with the change, something sinister enters the room. I conceal the evil with clothes that don't fit. A camouflage can sometimes feel like a security blanket.

Tego Says, "I'm Mas Monster"

The doctor asks me to bend down and touch my toes. They take various X-rays. The doctor explains to Mami there's a curvature in my back and it's called scoliosis. I immediately think of Judy Blume's novel *Deenie*, and I'm pissed off. Deenie in the book is white, so I just assumed a crooked back could happen only to white people. I didn't know scoliosis was a universal thing, a condition anyone could get. I feel Judy Blume has duped me.

"She'll have to be fitted for a back brace," the doctor says. "She'll have to wear it for a year or two."

Mami calculates how much this will cost. There are various appointments, and the only thing I'll remember later is the day we go to pick up the brace. My parents both come, dressed in their Sunday best, because talking to doctors always seems so important.

The doctor teases me: "Why are you so serious? It's not the end of the world."

I scowl even more. He doesn't know how I've already started covering my body. Now I will have the weight of plastic armor to remind me this ugly shape must be concealed.

I am allowed to take the brace off for only two hours a day. When I do, I caress my stomach, and the skin feels foreign to me.

Wisin & Yandel Declare Noche de Sexo

His name is Tito, and we are in his bedroom. His parents are gone for the day, shopping or attending church or something. It's been a few months since

I stopped wearing the back brace, and Tito is the first boy to pay me some attention. Or maybe he's the first boy I'm letting take notice. We are alone on his bed, and the window is open, so I can hear our friends playing outside. My heart races because I know what's going to happen next, because I've been wanting it to happen. He's gentle, but the room is way too bright.

"Can't we pull the curtains?" I ask.

Tito wants to see everything. He wants to see me. I want to hide under the sheets.

"Come here," he says.

Tito places me in front of the mirror and forces me to look at myself, and I can't. I stare at the floor. At his hands on my waist. At the dust accumulating in the corner of the bedroom. When he says he loves me, I believe his words are directed to another girl, not this girl.

But Ivy Queen Only Wants to Dance

I'm eighteen years old and a freshman in college. I hang out with a circle of badass girls. One more powerful than the next. They are from all over—New York, California, Chicago—and have shortened names we invented: La Sylvia, Tina, Tere, Mari. They drink too much, talk too loudly, take over spaces. On Fridays we head to the only club in the small college town we now call home. As we get ready to step out, I grab another oversized black T-shirt.

They yell at me, "Why are you hiding all of this?" They dress me in form-fitting skirts. They pull my hair away from my face.

In the club, they smoke and grind up on college boys and keep them wanting more. Soon I am also doing this. With each Friday night, I slowly shed my inhibitions. I turn to vintage shops and buy dresses that fit my hourglass shape. I look at mirrors and feel OK about what I see. Just OK. I'm not in love, not yet. In fact, I sometimes try to revert to hiding my now curvy body, but my friends won't allow me to. They remind me of my power. When I enter the club, I feel invincible. Sometimes I even feel beautiful.

MY FRIENDS REMIND ME OF MY POWER.

"Soy Caro" and Bad

"Why do you take so many selfies?" she asks.

The woman smiles. She's genuinely confused. She thinks I should dress way more conservatively and not show too much. That I definitely shouldn't take up too much space.

Later that night I post another selfie, a sexy one. One in which I look right at the camera and think of the many times I couldn't even look at myself. The woman hits the heart button because she's paying attention to me admiring myself. I keep taking selfies. I don't care. I love my cellulite, my stretches, my Puerto Rican ass, my broken nose, my Iris Chacón–esque breasts. I wear sequin skirts like Iris's and think, *Yes, I've arrived*. I make up for all those years of hiding and thinking I wasn't worth it. This body has transformed, and the negative remix in my head sometimes pops up to remind me of the past, but I quickly switch to another tune. I listen to Bad Bunny nonstop and stare at his gel nails, in awe of how things have changed.

I take another selfie and get into this bumping perreo.

FURTHER READING

There is no shortage of incredible books for readers who want to take an even deeper dive into the wild world of bodies. In the list below, you'll find some excellent fiction and nonfiction titles that explore the various aspects of having and operating a body.

For a fuller exploration of mental health and mental illness—which has been discussed throughout the book but has not been the focus of it—pick up *(Don't) Call Me Crazy: 33 Voices Start the Conversation about Mental Health*.

NONFICTION

Beauty Is a Verb: The New Poetry of Disability by Jennifer Bartlett, Sheila Black, Michael Northen

The Bite of the Mango by Mariatu Kamara

The Body Image Workbook for Teens by Julia V. Taylor

The Body Is Not an Apology by Sonya Renee Taylor

The Body Keeps the Score by Bessel van der Kolk

Taking Flight by Michaela DePrince

FICTION

Akata Witch and *Akata Warrior* by Nnedi Okorafor (albinism)

Bone Gap by Laura Ruby (face blindness)

Braced by Alyson Gerber (scoliosis)

El Deafo by Cece Bell (deafness)

Far from You by Tess Sharpe (chronic pain)

Five Flavors of Dumb by Antony John (deafness)

How We Roll by Natasha Friend (alopecia)

The Lake Effect by Erin McCahan (Crohn's disease)

The Last Leaves Falling by Fox Benwell (ALS)

North of Beautiful by Justina Chen (port-wine stain)

The One Thing by Marci Lyn Curtis (blindness)

Otherbound by Corinne Duyvis (mutism, amputation)

Out of My Mind by Sharon Draper (cerebral palsy)

Pinned by Sharon G. Flake (limb difference)

Run by Kody Keplinger (blindness)

Send Me a Sign by Tiffany Schmidt (cancer)

Shark Girl by Kelly Bingham (amputation)

Six of Crows by Leigh Bardugo (limp)

A Time to Dance by Padma Venkatraman (amputation)

Two Girls Staring at the Ceiling by Lucy Frank (Crohn's disease)

Unbroken edited by Marieke Nijkamp (all disabled main characters)

When I Was the Greatest by Jason Reynolds (Tourette's syndrome)

You're Welcome, Universe by Whitney Gardner (deafness)

ALSO CHECK OUT THESE
RAD BODY ACTIVISTS

Steve Post (whose "fat-in" in 1967 brought awareness to size discrimination)

Lew Louderback (whose 1967 *Saturday Evening Post* essay launched the fat acceptance movement)

Judy Freespirit and Aldebaran (founders of Fat Underground in 1972)

Tasha Fierce

Amy Pence Brown

Charlotte Cooper

Virgie Tovar

Corissa Enneking

Aarti Olivia Dubey

Evette Dionne

Miguel M. Morales

CONTRIBUTOR BIOS

TYRA BANKS is the supermodel, super entrepreneur, and super CEO of our time. As an original Victoria's Secret Angel, the first African American model to be featured on the cover of the *Sports Illustrated* swimsuit edition, and the creator/executive producer of one of the longest-running competition shows, *America's Next Top Model*, Tyra has made it her life's mission to expand the definition of beauty and empower women worldwide. In 2012, she graduated from the Owner/President Management program at Harvard Business School, and now she teaches personal branding at Stanford University's business school. She has been listed twice among *Time* magazine's "100 Most Influential People in the World."

KELLY BASTOW is a comic creator and illustrator from Newfoundland, Canada. Her work primarily features women and nature, and she also creates many autobiographical comics.

SHANE BURCAW is the author of two memoirs—*Laughing at My Nightmare* and *Strangers Assume My Girlfriend Is My Nurse*—and the picture book *Not So Different: What You Really Want to Ask about Having a Disability*. He is the founder of a nonprofit organization that provides adaptive technology to people living with muscular dystrophy. He and his fiancée, Hannah Aylward, are the duo behind the popular YouTube channel Squirmy and Grubs, which documents their interabled relationship. He and Hannah live in Minneapolis, Minnesota, with their pet rats, Ducky and Squirt.

ROSHANI CHOKSHI is the author of commercial and critically acclaimed books for middle-grade and young adult readers that transport audiences to fantastical worlds heavily inspired by world mythology and folklore. Her work has been nominated for Locus and Nebula awards and has frequently appeared on Best of the Year lists from Barnes & Noble, BuzzFeed, and more. Her *New York Times* bestselling series include the Star-Touched Queen duology, the Gilded Wolves, and Aru Shah and the End of Time, which was recently optioned for film by Paramount Pictures.

PATRICIA S. ELZIE (@theinfophile) is a researcher, writer, blogger, librarian, and podcaster. She spent many years as a sex educator and interpersonal-communication expert and still enjoys giving advice about sex, dating, and getting your life together. She lives with her wife in Oakland, California, where they both read and bake with large amounts of enthusiasm.

KATI GARDNER is the author of *Brave Enough* and *Finding Balance*. She is a childhood cancer survivor and amputee. She sadly doesn't watch *General Hospital* anymore. She lives in North Carolina with her family.

ALEX GINO is the author of the middle-grade novels *Rick*; *You Don't Know Everything, Jilly P!*; and the Stonewall Book Award–winning *George* (informally known as *Melissa's Story*). They love glitter, ice cream, gardening, awe-ful puns, and stories that reflect the diversity and complexity of being alive. Born and raised on Staten Island, New York, they now enjoy living in Oakland, California.

EUGENE GRANT is a writer and activist. He has been published in the *Guardian*, the *New Statesman*, and the *Independent* and has appeared in televised documentaries and debates. He lives in the UK with his partner.

I. W. GREGORIO is a practicing surgeon by day, masked avenging YA writer by night. A founding member of We Need Diverse Books, she is the author of *This Is My Brain in Love* and the Lambda Literary Award finalist *None of the Above*. She lives in Pennsylvania with her husband and two children.

GAVIN GRIMM is a twenty-year-old transgender-rights activist, best known as the plaintiff represented by the ACLU in *G. G. v. GCPSB*. Gavin is also nationally recognized as an advocate and educational speaker for the trans community. A trans man himself, Gavin has been advocating for the community since he was fifteen and banned from the boys' bathroom at his Virginia high school.

KATE HART is the author of *After the Fall* and a contributor to the anthologies *Toil and Trouble*, *Hope Nation*, and *Out Now*. After earning degrees in Spanish and history, Kate worked in early education and taught middle school, then wrote grants and marketing materials for a nonprofit serving adults with disabilities. She was also a weekly contributor to YA Highway, three-time pick for *Writer's Digest's* "101 Best Websites for Writers." Today she owns Natural State Treehouses with her spouse and sells woodworking and fiber arts at TheBadasserie.net. Kate is a citizen of the Chickasaw Nation, with Choctaw heritage, and lives with her family in Northwest Arkansas.

KELLY JENSEN is a former teen librarian who worked in several public libraries before pursuing a full-time career in writing and editing. Her current position is with *Book Riot* (bookriot.com), where she focuses on talking about young adult literature. Her books include *Here We Are: Feminism for the Real World* and *(Don't) Call Me Crazy*, a collection of art, essays, and words to launch a powerful and important conversation about mental health. It was named a best book of 2018 by the *Washington Post* and earned a Schneider Family Book Award Honor.

KATE BIGAM KAPUT is a writer, editor, and digital media strategist based in Cleveland, Ohio, where she lives with her husband, two cats, and a seemingly bottomless collection of books. She blogs at GreatestEscapist.com.

KIRAN GANDHI, who performs as Madame Gandhi, is an electronic-music artist and activist based in Los Angeles. She studied mathematics at Georgetown University and worked as the first-ever data analyst at Interscope Records before going on to receive her MBA from Harvard. Having gained recognition as the former drummer for the artist M.I.A. and as the viral free-bleeding runner at the 2015 London Marathon, Madame Gandhi now produces music that elevates and celebrates the female voice.

RACHAEL LIPPINCOTT is the #1 *New York Times* bestselling author of *Five Feet Apart*. She currently resides in Pittsburgh, Pennsylvania.

CAROLYN LONDON is a retired professional photographer; mother to Tyra Banks and her brother, Devin; the CEO emeritus of the Tyra Banks Company; and the cofounder of the TZONE Foundation. She has five grandchildren and two great-grandchildren.

AMANDA LOVELACE is the author of the celebrated Women Are Some Kind of Magic series. Somehow, she is also the two-time winner of the Goodreads Choice Award for best poetry, as well as a *USA Today* and *Publishers Weekly* bestselling author. When she isn't reading, writing, or drinking a much-needed cup of coffee, you can find her casting spells from her home in a (very) small town on the Jersey Shore.

ALICIA LUTES is a screenwriter, essayist, and cultural critic based in Los Angeles, California. She has written for Vulture, *Elle*, *Playboy*, MTV News, *Cosmopolitan*, *Stylist*, Well+Good, Bustle, and more. Previously, she was the managing editor at Nerdist, where she was also the creator and host of the web series *Fangirling*.

JOHN MCGINTY is an actor who happens to be Deaf and lives in both the English-speaking world and that of American Sign Language. He acted in two Broadway revivals and is an advocate for diversity and inclusion in the arts. He is excited to work with the next generation of people who are doing inclusive and diverse theater.

ANNA-MARIE MCLEMORE (they/them) was born in the foothills of the San Gabriel Mountains and taught by their family to hear La Llorona in the Santa Ana winds. Anna-Marie is the author of *The Weight of Feathers*, a finalist for the 2016 William C. Morris Debut Award; the 2017 Stonewall Honor Book *When the Moon Was Ours*, which was longlisted for the National Book Award for Young People's Literature and won the James Tiptree Jr. Award; *Wild Beauty*, a Kirkus Best Book of 2017; and *Blanca & Roja*, a *New York Times Book Review* Editors' Choice. Their latest is *Dark and Deepest Red*, a reimagining of *The Red Shoes* based on true medieval events.

D. M. MOEHRLE is a writer and librarian living in Ventura, California. She has written for the Rumpus, *Teen Vogue*, Shondaland.com, and other publications. You can follow her on social media: @loather.

JULIE MURPHY lives in North Texas with her husband, who loves her; her dog, who adores her; and her cats, who tolerate her. After several wonderful years in the library world, Julie now writes full-time. When she's not writing or reliving her reference-desk glory days, she can be found watching made-for-TV movies, hunting for the perfect slice of cheese pizza, and planning her next great travel adventure. She is also the #1 *New York Times* bestselling author of the young adult novels *Dumplin'* (now a film on Netflix), *Puddin'*, *Ramona Blue*, *Side Effects May Vary*, and *Faith: Taking Flight*. *Dear Sweet Pea* is her debut middle-grade novel.

JUNAUDA PETRUS-NASAH is a writer, pleasure activist, filmmaker, and performance artist born on Dakota land, of Black-Caribbean descent. Her work centers around wildness, queerness, Black-diasporic futurism, ancestral healing, sweetness, shimmer, and liberation. She lives in Minneapolis with her wife and family.

BENJAMIN PU is a 2020 campaign reporter for NBC News. When Ben isn't on the road, covering the election, he lives in New York City. He received his bachelor's degree from the University of California, Santa Barbara.

ALY RAISMAN is a gold-medal-winning Olympic gymnast who captained the US team to victories in 2012 and 2016. She has won six Olympic medals overall and was a member of two gold-medal-winning World Championships teams. Aly is a native of Needham, Massachusetts, and her love for the sport can be traced back to a "mommy and me" gymnastics class she took as an eighteen-month-old. Aly is a leader on and off the floor and is a fierce advocate for body positivity.

NAT RAZI is an environmental adviser, fantasy novelist, and amateur baker. She works as an editor at Disability in Kidlit and advocates for disability-inclusive environmental policy. She was living in New York City when this bio was written, but she never stays in one place for long.

LILLIAM RIVERA is the award-winning author of the young adult novels *Dealing in Dreams* and *The Education of Margot Sanchez*, both published by Simon & Schuster. Her work has appeared in the *Washington Post*, the *New York Times*, and *Elle*, to name a few. Lilliam lives in Los Angeles.

SARA SAEDI is a TV writer in Los Angeles. She currently writes for the CW show *Katy Keene*. She's also written three YA books, including her memoir, *Americanized: Rebel without a Green Card*. You can find her at SaraSaediWriter.com.

ABBY SAMS is a disabled activist and college student who enjoys public speaking and educating. She runs a small low-waste online store and uses her free time to do wheelchair races around the country in order to raise awareness for rare illnesses.

JOURDAIN SEARLES is a writer, performer, and cultural critic who hails from Augusta, Georgia, and currently resides in Queens, New York. She has written for many outlets, including Bitch Media, the AV Club, Vulture, and MTV News. Jourdain is feminist with a passion for empowering women and girls from marginalized communities.

Writer and body-positive activist **MARS SEBASTIAN** (better known as MarsinCharge on social media) aims to empower and encourage through her work. She believes that the self is a forever-shifting concept. She hopes you enjoy this collection and think of her piece in it as a representation of who she was at the time of its creation.

ERIC SMITH is a literary agent and author from Elizabeth, New Jersey. He's worked on award-winning and *New York Times* bestselling books, and when he isn't busy helping authors with their books, he sometimes writes his own. His latest novels include *The Girl and the Grove* and *Don't Read the Comments*. He lives in Philadelphia with his wife, son, and corgi. He still listens to musicals every single day but avoids Christmas music.

JERLYN M. THOMAS is a design director and product designer based in New York City. She creates digital experiences, concentrating on inclusivity and design accessibility. Her passion bridges the gap between technology and art to communicate with diverse audiences. She's also a published author and digital illustrator who posts art she draws during her commutes on her Instagram (@commuteartist) when she's not training for her next ultramarathon or triathlon.

KARA THOMAS is the author of the YA mysteries *The Darkest Corners*, *Little Monsters*, and *The Cheerleaders*, all published by Delacorte Press. You can find her reading Reddit's Unresolved Mysteries thread in the middle of the night.

LIBBY VANDERPLOEG is a Michigan-based artist, illustrator, and designer. Her client list includes Anthropologie, the *New York Times*, TED Talks, Penguin Books, the *New Yorker*, and Instagram, among others. She's had a lot of fun over the years seeing several of her animated GIFs go viral, including her "Lift Each Other Up" piece. When she's not drawing, she loves to bake, go for bike rides, run, and dig around in the garden.

ALICE WONG is a disabled activist, podcaster, and consultant based in San Francisco. She is the founder and director of the Disability Visibility Project, an online community dedicated to creating, sharing, and amplifying disability media and culture. Alice is also the editor of *Disability Visibility*, an anthology of essays by disabled people, coming out summer 2020 from Vintage Books. You can find her on Twitter: @SFdirewolf.

YAO XIAO was born in China and emigrated to the United States at age sixteen. She first studied fine art in Seattle and later at the Memphis College of Art, before moving to New York and enrolling in a BFA program at the School of Visual Arts. After graduation in 2013 with a degree in illustration, Yao sought a way to document her experiences as a queer immigrant and developed a series of comics incorporating illustration and writing. She continued to build on this practice and today is a successful illustrator, cartoonist, and writer. Yao's work has been featured in *BuzzFeed*, *Entertainment Weekly*, *National Geographic*, *Time*, and *Vice*, among others. Yao has shown her work at galleries in New York, San Francisco, and Seattle. Her first graphic novel is *Everything Is Beautiful, and I'm Not Afraid* from Andrews McMeel Publishing.

Acknowledgments

Every book is a different experience, and every book project has a different community that helps make it happen.

My community is the best.

Thank you to agent of wonder Tina Dubois, as well as Tamara Kawar. I'm forever grateful for my editor, Krestyna Lypen, and publisher, Elise Howard, along with the entire hardworking team at Algonquin Young Readers. You are all my dream team.

Thanks also to Katherine Sullivan for this seed of an idea years ago and enthusiasm for getting curious about everything. Alyssa Wees for accountability and writing dates that have become a highlight of my week. Eric Smith for off-the-record celebrations, humor, and encouragement. Bryce Kozla for your keen eye and insights about accessibility, both for this book and the greater world at large. As always, Liz Burns for being someone who always and forever understands me.

Woodstock, Illinois, is still new to me, but thanks to people like Rachel Bellavia, Lindsey DiCello, Arlene Lynes at Read Between the Lynes, Martha Hansen at Woodstock Public Library, and my teachers and peers at the Yoga Lounge, this has become such an incredible place to live, to write, and to thrive.

My mom and my grandma get thanked in every book for paying off the library fines I racked up as a teen. It's all on me now, and I know how bad I am about returning books on time.

Erik, you are my best friend and the love of my life. I'm glad we're doing this thing together and that we're one degree closer to being friends with Tyra Banks.

Last but not least, thank you to every single reader who has picked up one of my books or shared it with someone in their life. You are why I do this, and you are why I'll forever be grateful I get to do this.

COPYRIGHTS

Jennifer Brister

ABOUT THE EDITOR

KELLY JENSEN

is a former librarian and current editor at *Book Riot* and her own popular book blog, *Stacked*. She's the editor of two highly acclaimed YA anthologies, *Here We Are: Feminism for the Real World* and *(Don't) Call Me Crazy: 33 Voices Start the Conversation about Mental Health*. Her writing has been featured in *BUST* magazine, *Fortune*, *Bustle*, and more. When not working with words, she teaches yoga, hangs out with a motley crew of pets, and enjoys all the black licorice no one else wants.

Follow her on Instagram @heykellyjensen and her website kellybjensen.com.

LET'S GET TALKING!

KEEP THE CONVERSATION GOING!

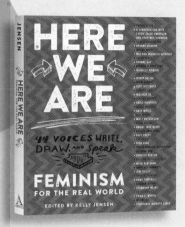

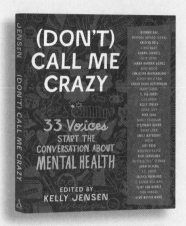

ISBN: 978-1-61620-586-7

ISBN: 978-1-61620-781-6

HERE WE ARE:
44 Voices Write, Draw, and Speak about Feminism for the Real World

(DON'T) CALL ME CRAZY:
33 Voices Start the Conversation about Mental Health

Writers, dancers, actors, and artists contribute essays, lists, poems, comics, and illustrations about everything from body positivity to romance to gender identity to intersectionality to the greatest girl friendships in fiction. Together, they share diverse perspectives on and insights into what feminism means and what it looks like.

To understand mental health, we need to talk openly about it. Because there's no single definition of *crazy*, there's no single experience that embodies it, and the word itself means different things—wild? extreme? disturbed? passionate?—to different people. If you've ever struggled with your mental health, or know someone who has, come on in, turn the pages . . . and let's get talking.

"*Here We Are* boldly and proudly passes the torch to the next generation of leaders." —*Teen Vogue*

"Jensen has brought together sharp and vivid perspectives. This book asks questions and provides real-life experiences and hope for the future." —*The Washington Post,* Best Children's Books of 2018